Student Workbook

From School to Work

J.J. Littrell, Ed. D.
Arizona State University
Tempe, Arizona

Annie Hunter Clasen
Instructor
Aparicio-Levy Technical Center
Tampa, Florida

Peggy Pearson
Diversified Career Technology Coordinator
Simmons Career Center
Plant City, Florida

Publisher
The Goodheart-Willcox Company, Inc.
Tinley Park, Illinois
www.g-w.com

Introduction

This *Student Workbook* is designed for use with the *From School to Work* text. As you complete the activities in this *Workbook*, you review the facts and concepts presented in the text. The overall objective of these activities is to help you make a smooth transition from your classroom to a meaningful job in the workplace.

The activities in this *Workbook* are divided into chapters corresponding to the chapters in the text. By reading the text first, you have the information needed to complete the activities. Try to complete each without referring to the text. Then check the text for answers to questions you could not complete. Compare your answers with the information in the text.

The activities will help you gain the skills you need to succeed in the workplace. Some activities, such as crossword puzzles, true/false questions, and math exercises, have "right" answers. Other activities ask you to evaluate various situations, make comparisons, or draw your own conclusions. These activities have neither "right" nor "wrong" answers since they are designed to stimulate creative thinking and help you develop ideas. Do your best to give thoughtful consideration to all your responses.

Contents

Part 3   Career Planning

Part 4 The Job Hunt

Part 5 Job Satisfaction

Part 6   Managing Your Income

Making the Transition from School to Work

Getting to Know Your Classmates

Activity A

Chapter 1

Name_____

Date_____Period_____

Interview someone in your class. Find the answers to the following questions and ask two questions of your own. Use the information to prepare an introduction that mentions five interesting facts about the person.

Name of classmate: _____

1. At what grade level are you? _____

2. How long have you been a student at this school? _____

3. What other schools have you attended? _____
   _____

4. Why did you choose to take this class? _____
   _____

5. Are you presently employed?_____ If so, where? _____
   _____

   A. How long have you worked there? _____

   B. What other employment or volunteer work have you done?_____
      _____

   C. How did you obtain your employment or volunteer work? _____
      _____

6. Do you have any hobbies or sports interests? _____
   _____

7. What do you do in your spare time?_____

8. What extracurricular activities were you involved in last year? Explain why you *were* or *were not* involved. _____
   _____

9. What extracurricular activities do you plan to pursue this school year? _____
   _____

10. What was your favorite movie in the past year? _____
    _____

(Continued)

Name_____

11. What was the most meaningful event for you this past year? _____

_____

12. What was the most embarrassing thing that ever happened to you? _____

_____

_____

13. What do you plan to do after graduation? _____

_____

14. What are your parents' or guardians' occupations? Briefly describe their jobs. _____

_____

_____

15. List three adjectives to describe yourself:

A. _____

B. _____

C. _____

16. Finish the following sentence: "If I had my choice, I'd take a job in_____

because_____

_____ .

17. Who has influenced you most and in what ways? _____

_____

18. Which two places would you like to visit?_____

_____

_____

19. Write two additional questions here and your responses.

Question: _____

Response:_____

_____

_____

Question: _____

Response:_____

_____

_____

Candidates for Work-Based Education

Activity B

Name_____

Chapter 1

Date_____ Period_____

Read two case studies about students who are candidates for work-based learning programs in their schools. From the information given in the text, explain how each student could benefit from a work-based learning program. Be prepared to discuss your responses in class.

Case 1. John wants to own his own landscape business someday. During his senior year, he can participate in a school-to-work experience in turf management at a local golf course. He is not sure the experience will help him. John asks your advice. What would you tell him?

_____

_____

_____

_____

_____

_____

_____

_____

_____

Case 2. Susan will be a senior this fall. After graduation she plans to go to college. She says she wants to major in veterinary medicine, but her best grades are not in science. If she could only get some experience at an animal clinic, she would be more certain of whether all the hard work required to become a veterinarian will result in a job she loves. Also, she needs a job now to earn money for college. How could a work-based learning program benefit Susan?

_____

_____

_____

_____

_____

_____

_____

_____

The School-to-Work Experience

Activity C

Chapter 1

Name_____

Date_____Period_____

Read the statements below and write the missing terms in the crossword puzzle.

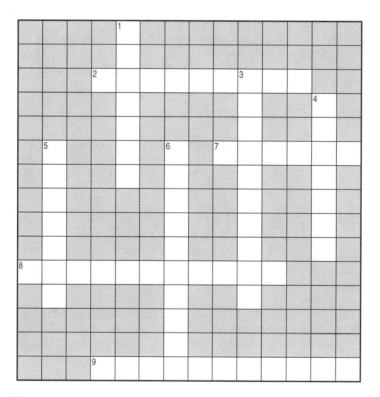

Across

2. School programs that prepare students for the workplace are called _____-_____ learning programs.

7. The coworker who will help you learn your new job is called the work-based _____.

8. The special teacher or counselor at school who assists students in a work-based learning program is known as the school-to-work _____.

9. A school program that alternates students between a paid job experience at a work site and time in the classroom is called _____ education.

Down

1. A work-based mentor is also called a training _____.

3. The _____ is your boss in the workplace.

4. The school-to-work coordinator is sometimes called the _____ coordinator.

5. The training _____ is the job site where a student works to learn job skills.

6. A program that offers paid or unpaid work experience to learn about a job or industry is an _____.

The Benefits of School-to-Work Programs

Activity D

Chapter 1

Name_____

Date_____Period_____

Ken graduated from East High School in June. The week after graduation, he was employed in a full-time job that offered an opportunity for advancement. He wrote the letter below to his former school-to-work coordinator. Read Ken's letter and answer the questions that follow.

---

612 W. Maple Drive
Newland, AZ 85011
June 20, 20XX

Dear Mr. Hudson:

It's only one week after graduation, and I have some good news to share with you. I already have a job as a technician at the Edison Electronic Company! It's a great job, and I even have a chance to be promoted if I get more training and do well on the job.

Actually, the reason I'm writing is to let you know that your Industrial Cooperative Education class helped me get the job. Your class meant a great deal to me. It gave me a chance to work in industrial electronics during my senior year.

I remember you told us that most adults spend much of their lives working. That made me realize a person's work should be a good experience. For that reason, I wanted to get some work experience before graduating from high school. I also wanted to find out if I would like electronics work. By participating in the school-to-work program, I found that I enjoyed the work very much. The work experience gave me a chance to apply some of the skills I learned in your electronics classes. By listening and learning on the job, I also gained new skills. Of course, earning a paycheck was nice, too!

That school-to-work experience was important for another reason—it gave me the feeling of being an important part of the workforce. I felt I was treated not just as a student, but also as an adult with a job that mattered. At the work site, I also learned to work with my supervisors and other employees.

I know my on-the-job experience in high school persuaded my current employer to hire me over other job applicants. I also know that my school-to-work experience will help me advance in the future.

Thank you for helping me.

Sincerely,

Ken McDaniel

Ken McDaniel

---

1. Why did Ken write to Mr. Hudson? _____

_____

_____

_____

(Continued)

Name_____

2. What high school subject did Mr. Hudson teach Ken? _____

_____

3. For what reason did Ken want to participate in the school-to-work program? _____

_____

_____

_____

4. Did Ken earn money during his school-to-work experience? _____

_____

5. Why did Ken feel adultlike in his school-to-work program? _____

_____

_____

6. List five benefits Ken received from his on-the-job experience. _____

_____

_____

_____

_____

_____

7. Imagine you are Ken's current employer. Write a letter to Mr. Hudson explaining why you hired a high school graduate with work-based learning experience. _____

_____

_____

_____

_____

_____

_____

_____

_____

_____

_____

_____

_____

_____

What Are Your Workplace Skills?

Activity E

Chapter 1

Name_____

Date_____ Period_____

Review the knowledge and skills in the chart and rate your workplace readiness by checking the appropriate box for each. Then answer the questions that follow.

Workplace Skills	Very Good	Good	Fair	Poor	Do Not Possess
Academic Foundations					
Read and comprehend written material.					
Compose neat and accurately written messages.					
Calculate a percentage discount on an item.					
Apply basic measurement methods.					
Correctly demonstrate common lab or workshop procedures.					
Communications					
Make oral presentations well.					
Write an effective letter.					
Listen to instructions to complete a new task.					
Use nonverbal communication well.					
Summarize complex facts into charts and diagrams.					
Problem Solving and Critical Thinking					
Prioritize work assignments.					
Apply established procedures to new projects.					
Identify problems and form possible answers.					
Compare and evaluate alternative solutions.					
Form new, creative approaches to challenges.					
Information Technology Applications					
Use a computer to create various documents and diagrams.					
Research and collect data from reliable Internet sources.					
Organize, maintain, and transfer computer files correctly.					
Use presentation software for effective communications.					
Use spreadsheet and database applications correctly.					
Systems					
Explain and draw an organizational chart.					
Diagram the steps of a problem's possible solutions.					
Monitor, correct, and improve your work performance.					
Break down a complex task into component parts.					
Understand roles within teams and work units.					
Safety, Health, and Environment					
Know and follow all safety rules.					
Wear personal protective equipment.					
Identify common safety hazards and emergency procedures they require.					
Identify personal behaviors that are unsafe.					
Educate others to health and safety awareness.					
Leadership and Teamwork					
Contribute to positive group efforts.					
Teach others new work skills.					
Eliminate barriers in work relationships.					
Negotiate to gain an agreement.					
Work well with others from different cultures.					

(Continued)

Name_____

Workplace Skills	Very Good	Good	Fair	Poor	Do Not Possess
Ethics and Legal Responsibilities					
Distinguish between ethical and unethical conduct at work.					
Explain plagiarism.					
Identify when permission is needed before certain information is used.					
Name the laws that regulate your workplace.					
Identify situations that may pose legal problems.					
Employability and Career Development					
Develop a career plan.					
Know and understand the value of transferable skills.					
Explain the qualifications needed before entering the career of your choice.					
Identify the importance of workplace dress and appearance standards.					
Explain what you must do to get a promotion.					
Technical Skills					
Judge the best procedures, tools, or machines to use.					
Examine new technology's impact on your work.					
Operate equipment according to guidelines.					
Identify reasons for wrong results from tools or machines.					
Follow maintenance procedures to prevent failures.					

How can you improve the *Fair* or *Poor* skills you identified?

_____

_____

_____

_____

How can you acquire the skills you do *not* possess?

_____

_____

_____

_____

How will your skills influence your career choice?

_____

_____

_____

_____

2 Understanding Work-Based Learning

Training Agreement Responsibilities

Activity A

Chapter 2

Name _____

Date _____ Period _____

After reviewing a copy of the work-based learning training agreement used by your school, summarize in your own words the responsibilities required of each person who signs the agreement.

1. Employer's responsibilities: _____

   _____

   _____

   _____

   _____

   _____

   _____

   _____

   _____

   _____

   _____

   _____

   _____

   _____

   A. Which responsibility do you think is the most important? Why? _____

   _____

   _____

   _____

   B. How important are the other responsibilities the employer has after signing the agreement? _____

   _____

   _____

(Continued)

Name_____

2. Your responsibilities: _____

_____

_____

_____

_____

_____

_____

_____

_____

   A. Which responsibility do you think is most important? Why? _____

_____

_____

   B. How important are the other responsibilities you have after signing the agreement? _____

_____

_____

3. Program coordinator's responsibilities: _____

_____

_____

_____

4. Parent's or guardian's responsibilities: _____

_____

_____

_____

5. What is the purpose of the training agreement?_____

_____

_____

_____

_____

_____

_____

_____

Getting a Social Security Card

Activity B

Chapter 2

Name _____

Date _____ Period _____

Complete the application for a social security card by filling in every item that applies to you.

SOCIAL SECURITY ADMINISTRATION
Application for a Social Security Card

Form Approved
OMB No. 0960-0066

		First	Full Middle Name	Last
1	**NAME** TO BE SHOWN ON CARD			
	FULL NAME AT BIRTH IF OTHER THAN ABOVE	First	Full Middle Name	Last
	OTHER NAMES USED			

2 MAILING ADDRESS Do Not Abbreviate

Street Address, Apt. No., PO Box, Rural Route No.

City | State | ZIP Code

3 CITIZENSHIP (Check One)

☐ U.S. Citizen ☐ Legal Alien Allowed To Work ☐ Legal Alien **Not** Allowed To Work (See Instructions On Page 2) ☐ Other (See Instructions On Page 2)

4 SEX

☐ Male ☐ Female

5 RACE/ETHNIC DESCRIPTION (Check One Only - Voluntary)

☐ Asian, Asian-American or Pacific Islander ☐ Hispanic ☐ Black (Not Hispanic) ☐ North American Indian or Alaskan Native ☐ White (Not Hispanic)

6 DATE OF BIRTH Month, Day, Year

7 PLACE OF BIRTH (Do Not Abbreviate) City | State or Foreign Country | FCI

Office Use Only

8

A. MOTHER'S NAME AT HER BIRTH First | Full Middle Name | Last Name At Her Birth

B. MOTHER'S SOCIAL SECURITY NUMBER (See instructions for 8B on Page 2) └┴┴┘ - └┴┘ - └┴┴┴┘

9

A. FATHER'S NAME First | Full Middle Name | Last

B. FATHER'S SOCIAL SECURITY NUMBER (See instructions for 9B on Page 2) └┴┴┘ - └┴┘ - └┴┴┴┘

10 Has the applicant or anyone acting on his/her behalf ever filed for or received a Social Security number card before?

☐ Yes (If "yes", answer questions 11-13.) ☐ No (If "no," go on to question 14.) ☐ Don't Know (If "don't know," go on to question 14.)

11 Enter the Social Security number previously assigned to the person listed in item 1. └┴┴┘ - └┴┘ - └┴┴┴┘

12 Enter the name shown on the most recent Social Security card issued for the person listed in item 1.

First | Middle Name | Last

13 Enter any different date of birth if used on an earlier application for a card.

Month, Day, Year

14 TODAY'S DATE Month, Day, Year

15 DAYTIME PHONE NUMBER ( ) - Area Code | Number

I declare under penalty of perjury that I have examined all the information on this form, and on any accompanying statements or forms, and it is true and correct to the best of my knowledge.

16 YOUR SIGNATURE

17 YOUR RELATIONSHIP TO THE PERSON IN ITEM 1 IS:

☐ Self ☐ Natural Or Adoptive Parent ☐ Legal Guardian ☐ Other (Specify)

DO NOT WRITE BELOW THIS LINE (FOR SSA USE ONLY)

NPN			DOC	NTI	CAN		ITV
PBC	EVI	EVA	EVC	PRA	NWR	DNR	UNIT

EVIDENCE SUBMITTED

SIGNATURE AND TITLE OF EMPLOYEE(S) REVIEW-ING EVIDENCE AND/OR CONDUCTING INTERVIEW

_____ DATE

DCL _____ DATE

The Training Plan

Activity C

Chapter 2

Name _____

Date _____ Period _____

Complete the training plan cover page below. Use O*NET™, The Occupational Information Network (www.online.onetcenter.org) to locate your job title, number, and description. Then compare the job description given on O*NET with your present job responsibilities. Based on this comparison, prepare a short job description for your present job.

Training Plan for Work-Based Learning

Student's Name _____

Social Security No. _____ Home Phone_____

Student's Career Objective_____

Employer _____

Employer's Address _____

Dates of Employment _____

Supervisor _____

Job Title and Number (O*NET) _____

Job Description_____

_____

_____

_____

_____

_____

_____

_____

We agree that the tasks, duties, and/or competencies identified here will be included in the training plan for the student's training while enrolled in the Work-Based Learning Program.

Employer _____ Date_____

Program Coordinator_____ Date_____

Student_____ Date_____

Know the Law

Activity D	Name _____
Chapter 2	Date _____ Period _____

Read the following cases. Then answer the questions below and provide explanations.

Case 1. Wayne has been employed as a trainee in a print shop for one month and receives less than minimum wage for his work. According to the FLSA, have Wayne's rights been violated? _____

_____

Case 2. Karen and Don work for an insurance company. They were hired at the same time and do the same jobs. One day, Don found out that Karen was paid more for her work. Have Don's rights been violated?

_____

What should Don do? _____

Case 3. Linda works as a telephone operator for $9.00 an hour. One week she worked 48 hours. According to the FLSA, is Linda entitled to overtime pay? _____

_____

Assuming overtime is paid at a rate of 1½ times the regular rate for each hour worked beyond 40, what is Linda's pay for the week?

Case 4. Jamilla and Bill work in a large department store doing the same job with the same responsibilities. Jamilla has worked there for one year, while Bill has worked there for nine years. Jamilla found out Bill is paid a wage higher than hers. Were Jamilla's rights violated? _____

_____

Case 5. Wu has been employed at a card shop for three years. She works 40 hours per week, receiving less than minimum wage for her work. According to the FLSA, have Wu's rights been violated? _____

_____

What should she do? _____

Case 6. Sherry is 16 years old and works in the office of a large meatpacking plant. She would prefer to operate a meat-cutting machine, but the plant supervisor refuses to give her the job. According to the FLSA, have Sherry's rights been violated? _____

_____

Case 7. Hasem is a server in a restaurant. He is paid $5.50 per hour. According to the FLSA, have Hasem's rights been violated? _____

_____

_____

Case 8. Montel is 16 years old and in a job training program to become a customer service representative. He makes $5.00 per hour. According to the FLSA, have Montel's rights been violated? _____

_____

Case 9. Renalia is 18 years old. She works in a supermarket deli. She uses a meat and cheese slicer every day. According to the FLSA, have Renalia's rights been violated? _____

_____

Your Study Habits

Activity E

Chapter 2

Name_____

Date_____Period_____

Think about your study habits. Respond to the statements below, then analyze your responses. (There are no right or wrong answers.)

Yes	No	Sometimes	
_____	_____	_____	1. When it's time to study, I cannot seem to get started.
_____	_____	_____	2. I find it easy to keep my mind on what I am studying.
_____	_____	_____	3. I reread a line two or three times to get the meaning.
_____	_____	_____	4. I do not understand the words that I read.
_____	_____	_____	5. I like to read.
_____	_____	_____	6. I do not remember what I read.
_____	_____	_____	7. I do not take very good notes.
_____	_____	_____	8. I like to write.
_____	_____	_____	9. I usually do not know the assignment.
_____	_____	_____	10. I do not want to ask for help.
_____	_____	_____	11. I study with music playing.
_____	_____	_____	12. I like to participate in class.
_____	_____	_____	13. I use class time to socialize with my friends.
_____	_____	_____	14. When taking notes in class, I write down every word the teacher says.
_____	_____	_____	15. When taking notes in class, I write down the most important points to help me remember the main ideas and facts.
_____	_____	_____	16. I keep a separate notebook for each class.
_____	_____	_____	17. I usually do the easiest assignments first.
_____	_____	_____	18. I complete class assignments every day.
_____	_____	_____	19. I make a list of tasks I must complete each day.
_____	_____	_____	20. I put the most important tasks to be done first on my list.

Explain what your answers to these statements reveal about your study habits.

_____

_____

_____

What steps could you take to improve your study habits?

_____

_____

_____

Organizing Your Schedule

Activity F　　　　　　　　　　　　Name_____

Chapter 2　　　　　　　　　　　　Date_____Period_____

As a work-based learning student, you will probably need to adjust your schedule in order to meet the required hours at school and at work. Use the chart below to keep track of how you spend your weekday time. Chart the time you spend at school, at work, studying, sleeping, and doing other activities throughout the day. Then analyze the finished chart and answer the following questions. (Be prepared to discuss how this activity helped you.)

Time	Monday	Tuesday	Wednesday	Thursday	Friday

(Continued)

Name_____

1. How many hours during the week did you spend

   in class? _____   sleeping? _____

   at work? _____   commuting? _____

   studying? _____   other? _____

2. What are your time wasters? _____

   _____

   _____

3. If you could eliminate (or reduce) one time waster from the chart, which one would it be? Explain. ____

   _____

   _____

4. How much uninterrupted time do you have for

   important tasks?_____

   yourself? _____

5. Do you have any free time to spend as you please? Explain. _____

   _____

6. Are you allowing yourself enough time to study? Explain. _____

   _____

7. Are you getting enough rest? Explain. _____

   _____

8. For which important activity can you never seem to find enough time? _____

   _____

9. How might you be able to make time for important activities? _____

   _____

   _____

   _____

   _____

10. What does *organizing your schedule in order of priority* mean? _____

    _____

11. How can an organized schedule give you more free time?_____

    _____

    _____

12. What changes, if any, would you make in your weekday schedule?_____

    _____

    _____

What Your Employer Expects

An Employer's View

Activity A   Name_____

Chapter 3   Date_____Period_____

Interview an employer to obtain answers to the following questions and directions. Discuss the interview in class.

1. What do you expect of an employee? _____

   _____

2. How important is it for an employee to have good attendance on the job? _____

   _____

3. List at least three good qualities an employee should have. _____

   _____

   _____

4. List at least three bad habits an employee should avoid. _____

   _____

   _____

5. In what ways does attitude affect an employee's job performance?_____

   _____

6. Define *employee loyalty.* _____

   _____

7. How are employees expected to dress while on the job?_____

   _____

8. How can having courteous employees in the workplace benefit your business?_____

   _____

9. What should an employee do after finishing an assigned job?_____

   _____

10. For what reasons would you fire an employee? _____

    _____

11. Describe the perfect employee. _____

    _____

    _____

12. How important is teamwork at your workplace? _____

    _____

    _____

Personal Qualities on the Job

Activity B   Name_____

Chapter 3   Date_____Period_____

Imagine you are an employer. Which of the following employee work traits would be most important to you and your business? Work with a group to rank the following employee traits in order of importance, with *1* most important and *15* least important. Then report your group's top five choices to the class.

_____ confidentiality

_____ cooperation

_____ courtesy

_____ excellent job performance

_____ good attendance

_____ good health and fitness

_____ honesty

_____ initiative

_____ loyalty

_____ neat personal appearance

_____ organizational skills

_____ positive attitude

_____ punctuality

_____ receptive to constructive criticism

_____ strong work ethic

_____ teamwork skills

What other personal qualities might an employer desire in an employee that are not listed above?_____

_____

_____

_____

_____

_____

_____

_____

_____

_____

_____

Personal Traits

Activity C

Chapter 3

Name_____

Date_____Period_____

Complete the puzzle by writing the correct personal traits in the spaces. Use the definitions below for clues.

1 ____ ____ ____ P ____ ____ ____ ____ ____ ____ ____
2 ____ ____ ____ E ____ ____ ____ ____ ____
3 ____ ____ ____ ____ ____ R ____ ____ ____ ____ ____
4 ____ ____ ____ ____ S ____ ____
5 ____ ____ ____ ____ O ____ ____ ____ ____ ____ ____
6 ____ ____ ____ ____ N ____ ____ ____ ____
7 ____ ____ ____ A ____ ____ ____
8 ____ ____ ____ L ____ ____
9 ____ ____ ____ ____ T ____ ____ ____
10 ____ ____ ____ R ____ ____ ____
11 ____ A ____ ____ ____ ____ ____ ____ ____
12 ____ ____ ____ ____ ____ I ____ ____ ____ ____ ____
13 ____ ____ ____ ____ ____ T ____ ____ ____
14 ____ ____ ____ ____ ____–____ S ____ ____ ____ ____

Definitions:

1. To be accountable

2. How you look

3. To get along with your coworkers and supervisor

4. Integrity; being truthful

5. To put forth your best effort and do a job well

6. Someone who is reliable

7. Being faithful to your employer

8. Mental and physical condition

9. Being on time

10. Showing good manners

11. An outlook on life

12. Finding tasks to do without being told

13. How much effort you put into your work

14. How you see yourself

Dependability and Work Ethic

Activity D	**Name**_____
Chapter 3	**Date**_____**Period**_____

Read the following story about Joseph. Then answer the questions below.

Joseph was hired by Mr. Johnson as a stocker in a grocery store. His job responsibilities included unloading boxes from delivery trucks and stocking the store shelves, refrigerators, and freezers. One Tuesday morning, Joseph unloaded some boxes of frozen food products from a delivery truck, but didn't follow his employer's directions to transfer the food to the freezer quickly. Mr. Johnson had explained that frozen food cannot be allowed to thaw. Joseph, however, became distracted by some of his friends who came to the store to talk with him. At noon, Joseph was hungry so he left for lunch without asking permission. He decided to handle important personal business instead of returning to work that afternoon. When Joseph arrived at work Wednesday morning, he was surprised to learn that Mr. Johnson had fired him and hired a replacement.

1. Was Mr. Johnson justified in firing Joseph? Explain. _____

_____

_____

_____

_____

2. If you were Mr. Johnson, what would you have said to Joseph on Wednesday? _____

_____

_____

_____

_____

3. What should Joseph have done about his friends distracting him from his work?_____

_____

_____

_____

_____

4. What should Joseph have done about his personal business? _____

_____

_____

_____

_____

Employer Job Evaluation

Activity E	Name_____
Chapter 3	Date_____Period_____

Evaluate your job performance from the viewpoint of an employer by placing a check in the appropriate spaces. Then answer the questions that follow.

1. Cooperation
_____ A Gets along well with others; is friendly with others.
_____ B Cooperates willingly; gets along with others.
_____ C Usually gets along with others.
_____ D Does not work well with others.
_____ E Is antagonistic; pulls against rather than works with others.

2. Initiative
_____ A Is resourceful; looks for tasks to learn and do.
_____ B Is fairly resourceful; does well by himself/herself.
_____ C Does routine work acceptably.
_____ D Takes very little initiative; requires urging.
_____ E Takes no initiative; has to be instructed repeatedly.

3. Courtesy
_____ A Is very courteous and very considerate of others.
_____ B Is considerate and courteous.
_____ C Usually is polite and considerate of others.
_____ D Is not particularly courteous in action or speech.
_____ E Has been discourteous to the public and staff.

4. Attitude Toward Constructive Criticism
_____ A Accepts criticism and improves greatly.
_____ B Accepts criticism and improvement noted.
_____ C Accepts criticism and tries to do better.
_____ D Doesn't pay much attention to criticism.
_____ E Doesn't profit by criticism; resents it.

5. Knowledge of Job
_____ A Knows job well and shows desire to learn more.
_____ B Understands work; needs little supervision.
_____ C Has learned necessary routine but needs supervision.
_____ D Pays little attention to learning job.
_____ E Has not tried to learn.

6. Accuracy of Work
_____ A Very seldom makes errors; does work of very good quality.
_____ B Makes few errors; is careful, thorough, and neat.
_____ C Makes errors; shows average care, thoroughness, and neatness.
_____ D Is frequently inaccurate and careless.
_____ E Is extremely careless.

7. Work Accomplished
_____ A Is fast and efficient; production is well above average.
_____ B Works rapidly; output is above average.
_____ C Works with ordinary speed; work is generally satisfactory.
_____ D Is slower than average.
_____ E Is very slow; output is unsatisfactory.

(Continued)

8. Work Habits

_____ A Is industrious; concentrates very well.
_____ B Seldom wastes time; is reliable.
_____ C Wastes time occasionally; is usually reliable.
_____ D Frequently wastes time; needs close supervision.
_____ E Habitually wastes time; has to be watched and reminded of work.

9. Adaptability

_____ A Learns quickly; is adept at meeting changing conditions.
_____ B Adjusts readily.
_____ C Makes necessary adjustments after considerable instruction.
_____ D Is slow in grasping ideas; has difficulty adapting to new situations.
_____ E Can't adjust to changing situations.

10. Personal Appearance

_____ A Is excellent in appearance; always looks neat.
_____ B Is very good in appearance; looks neat most of the time.
_____ C Is passable in appearance but should make effort to improve.
_____ D Often neglects appearance.
_____ E Is extremely careless in appearance.

11. Punctuality

_____ A Never tardy except for unavoidable emergencies.
_____ B Seldom tardy.
_____ C Punctuality could be improved.
_____ D Very often tardy.
_____ E Too frequently tardy.

12. Dependability

_____ A Never absent except for an unavoidable emergency.
_____ B Dependable.
_____ C Usually dependable.
_____ D Not regular enough in attendance.
_____ E Too frequently absent.

1. Do you believe this is an accurate evaluation of your work habits and performance? Explain. _____
_____

_____

2. In which areas could you improve? Explain. _____

_____

3. Which areas are your strongest? Why? _____

_____

4. Based on this evaluation, do you think you are a desirable employee? Explain. _____

_____

_____

5. In your opinion, what are three cases of employee absence that deserve to be excused? _____

_____

_____

Teamwork and Problem-Solving Skills

Handling Problems in Teams

Activity A	Name_____
Chapter 4	Date_____Period_____

Effective teams work together to address problems that occur among members. In order to keep a team working effectively, what would you say or do to a team member in the following situations?

Problem Behavior

What would you say or do?

1. Is always late.

2. Frequently starts side conversations during discussions.

3. Acts offended if his or her recommendations are not followed.

4. Rushes through to a quick decision to end a discussion.

5. Monopolizes the discussion.

6. Leaves before the job is done.

7. Brings personal problems to work.

8. Constantly tells jokes and keeps the team from working.

9. Refuses to work with another team member.

10. Gives lengthy, time-wasting explanations.

11. Suddenly turns silent.

12. Won't share the leadership role.

Using a Chart as a Scheduling Tool

Activity B　　　　　　　　　Name_____

Chapter 4　　　　　　　　　Date_____Period_____

Working in a team, plan the fund-raising event described below. Then use the chart outline at the bottom of the page to develop a Gantt chart for planning, executing, and evaluating the fund-raiser. If necessary, refer to the Gantt chart in your text.

　　"Spring Break" T-Shirt Fund-Raising Event: Imagine that your group is the club committee responsible for the entire fund-raising event. Your club advisor has instructed that the fund-raiser—from start to finish—should take no more than eight weeks. During that period, your team must create the shirt's design; find a shirt manufacturer and select colors; find a printer; determine production costs and selling price; take orders; collect money; and distribute the shirts. Your committee, as well as all other club members, will sell the T-shirts during a two-week period. After the sales period, you must finalize financial records and give a report to your club.

Planning Guide for T-Shirt Fund-Raising								
Task	**Week 1**	**Week 2**	**Week 3**	**Week 4**	**Week 5**	**Week 6**	**Week 7**	**Week 8**

Let's Work as a Team

Activity C   Name_____

Chapter 4   Date_____ Period_____

Work with three or four classmates to develop a car-buying chart as described below. Begin the group project by establishing team roles and brainstorming how to set up the chart. As a group, present your completed chart to the class. Work alone to answer the questions that follow.

Team Project: Creating a Car-Buying Guide

Assume your team works in a car-buying assistance department of a large travel club. Customers call your information line for help in deciding which new vehicles to purchase. Your department manager has asked your team to help this decision-making process by designing a chart that shows the following categories:

- types of vehicles available, such as compact/small, medium, large/luxury, minivans, sport-utility vehicles, convertibles, and pickups
- important buying information, such as safety features, miles-per-gallon rating, price ranges, equipment options, seating capacity, special awards, and results of collision tests
- other information your team feels is valuable

Research the information needed by checking consumer magazines, buying guides, newspapers, car specialty magazines, and the Internet. Design the chart on a large piece of paper or poster board. Indicate what types of pictures should be shown where.

---

1. What occurred among the members of your team during the following stages?

   A. Forming stage: _____

   _____

   _____

   _____

   B. Storming stage: _____

   _____

   _____

   _____

   C. Norming stage: _____

   _____

   _____

   _____

   D. Performing stage: _____

   _____

   _____

   _____

(Continued)

Name_____

2. Which team members fit each of the following roles?

   Leader(s):_____

   _____

   _____

   Encourager(s):_____

   _____

   _____

   Taskmaster(s):_____

   _____

   _____

   Critic(s): _____

   _____

   _____

   Recorder: _____

   _____

   _____

3. How did your team resolve any disagreements that occurred?

   _____

   _____

   _____

   _____

4. Which characteristics of an effective team developed within your group during the project?

   _____

   _____

   _____

   _____

5. What ideas resulted from the group's brainstorming sessions?

   _____

   _____

   _____

   _____

Team Problem-Solving Case Study

Activity D

Chapter 4

Name_____

Date_____ Period_____

In teams of five, review the following case study. Then use the problem-solving steps that follow to assist your team and solve the problem.

> **Case Study:** World Class Café, a restaurant specializing in international cuisine, seats 70 customers. It is open every day for lunch and dinner. Weekend nights are always busy, with the wait time often being an hour. Many of the customers are repeat customers. On a typical weekend night, the front room is fully staffed with one hostess, five waiters, and two busers. There is one manager on duty for both the front room and the kitchen areas.
>
> This Saturday night, a nearby company has reserved half the seats for a party from 6 p.m. to 9 p.m. On Thursday, two waiters and one buser have notified the manager that they cannot work this weekend. The manager calls a meeting of the front-room staff to develop a Saturday action plan for the work team. The front-room staff must address the staffing problem and be prepared to handle possible complaints about prices, food quality, and/or service.

Step 1: Identify and analyze the problem.

What is the problem?

_____

_____

_____

What criteria would you consider?

_____

_____

_____

_____

What constraints would you consider?

_____

_____

_____

_____

Step 2: Collect and analyze data.

What do you need to know about the problem that you do not already know?

_____

_____

_____

What information is available to you to help you solve this problem?

_____

_____

(Continued)

Name_____

Step 3: Consider possible solutions.

What are some possible solutions developed by your team through brainstorming?

_____

_____

_____

_____

_____

_____

_____

_____

_____

Step 4: Choose the best plan.

Considering your answers in Step 1, which plan seems best?

_____

_____

_____

_____

Step 5: Implement the plan.

What clues might indicate that the plan is (is not) working?

_____

_____

_____

_____

Step 6: Observe, evaluate, and adjust.

If this plan fails, what would your team recommend doing next time?

_____

_____

_____

What aids to problem solving did your team use? Give details.

_____

_____

_____

Teamwork and Problem-Solving Terms

Activity E

Chapter 4

Name_____

Date_____ Period_____

Match the following chapter terms with their definitions by writing the correct letter in each blank. Then answer the questions that follow.

_____ 1. A cross-trained group that has all members able to perform all duties.

_____ 2. The stage of team development when individuals are first grouped together.

_____ 3. What a company tries to achieve by meeting and exceeding customer expectations.

_____ 4. A team that has full responsibility for carrying out its assignment.

_____ 5. When all members of a group fully accept and support a decision.

_____ 6. The highest stage of team development.

_____ 7. A team consisting of workers from different areas who are grouped together to work on a specific project.

_____ 8. The process of making an expectation a reality.

_____ 9. Factors that may restrict your ability to solve a problem.

_____10. A pattern that is typical in the development of a social group.

_____11. A hostile situation resulting from opposing views.

_____12. A timetable graph used to help teams stay focused.

_____13. The stage of team development where disagreements are likely to occur.

_____14. A team with members of similar skills who are not able to perform one another's jobs.

_____15. A group technique used to develop many ideas in a short time.

_____16. The standards you use to find the best solution in problem solving.

_____17. A small group of people working together for a common purpose.

_____18. The objective that you want to attain.

A. team

B. quality

C. functional team

D. cross-functional team

E. self-directed team

F. multifunctional team

G. norm

H. Gantt chart

I. forming stage

J. storming stage

K. performing stage

L. goal

M. problem solving

N. criteria

O. constraints

P. brainstorming

Q. consensus

R. conflict

19. What does *working for a common good* mean? _____

_____

_____

20. When is humor beneficial to a team? _____

_____

(Continued)

Name_____

21. What methods could a team use to stay focused on its mission?_____

_____

_____

_____

22. What example of team conflict have you witnessed? (How was it resolved?) _____

_____

_____

_____

_____

23. What could have been done differently by the team described in Item 22 to prevent team conflict?_____

_____

_____

_____

24. For the teams on which you have served, what roles did the teams play? (Indicate below)

Team Name/Description	Functional	Cross-Functional	Self-Directed	Multifunctional
At school:_____	❑	❑	❑	❑
_____	❑	❑	❑	❑
At work: _____	❑	❑	❑	❑
_____	❑	❑	❑	❑
In sports: _____	❑	❑	❑	❑
_____	❑	❑	❑	❑
Other/volunteer: _____	❑	❑	❑	❑
_____	❑	❑	❑	❑

 **Communicating on the Job**

Effective Communication

Activity A

Chapter 5

Name_____

Date_____Period_____

Effective communication skills are necessary in the workplace and will improve your job performance. Prepare a written message in a word processing program and exchange your message with a partner. Then evaluate your own communication skills by answering the questions below. Share the evaluation with the class.

1. Who was the sender of the message? _____

2. What was the encoder? _____

3. What was the message?_____

4. What was the channel? _____

5. Who was the receiver?_____

6. What was the decoder? _____

7. Was there any feedback? _____ If so, what was it?_____

_____

8. Was there any noise? _____ If so, what was it? _____

_____

9. Did effective communication occur? _____ Why or why not? _____

_____

10. Based on your answers to these questions, describe yourself as a communicator. _____

_____

_____

_____

_____

11. What can you do to become a more effective communicator? _____

_____

_____

_____

_____

How Well Do You Listen?

Activity B   Name _____

Chapter 5   Date _____ Period _____

How well do you listen? Think about the conversations you have with others, including family members, teachers, and friends. Respond to the following statements by checking the response that best describes your behavior. Then analyze your responses.

Often   Sometimes   Never

_____   _____   _____   1. Are you distracted by others talking nearby?

_____   _____   _____   2. Do you continue to listen even though you think you know what is going to be said?

_____   _____   _____   3. Do you continue to listen even when you disagree with what is said?

_____   _____   _____   4. Do you have difficulty hearing the speaker?

_____   _____   _____   5. Does a speaker who does not make eye contact distract you?

_____   _____   _____   6. Do you continue to listen even though the speaker uses words you do not understand?

_____   _____   _____   7. Does your mind wander during a conversation?

_____   _____   _____   8. Do you interrupt others while they are talking?

_____   _____   _____   9. Do you ask the speaker to explain things you do not understand?

_____   _____   _____   10. Do you have trouble listening when others speak?

Based on your answers to these questions, describe yourself as a listener. _____

_____

_____

_____

_____

_____

_____

_____

Describe your major concerns about your listening skills. _____

_____

_____

_____

_____

_____

_____

_____

Parts of Business Letters

Name_____

Date_____Period_____

Identify the eight standard parts indicated on the business letter below.

A.

H. B. Jones Welding
812 N. 7th Avenue
Kansas City, Missouri 65100

B.

November 15, 20xx

C.

Acme Welding Supply
999 Camden St.
St. Louis, MO 63000

D.

Dear Sir or Madam:

E.

Please send me information about the new Acme welding machines you advertised in the *Welding Journal* last
month. My company rebuilds heavy road construction
equipment, and we need to replace five of our welding
machines.

If you have a salesperson in the Kansas City area, we
would appreciate having him or her call on us.

F.

Sincerely,

G.

Jackie Jones

Jackie Jones
Purchaser

H.

JRJ/ra

A. _____
   _____
B. _____
C. _____
   _____
D. _____
E. _____
F. _____
   _____
G. _____
H. _____
   _____

Complete the following statement: Neatness is important when writing a business letter because _____

_____

_____

_____

_____

Writing a Business Letter

Activity D   Name_____

Chapter 5   Date_____Period_____

In the space below, write a letter ordering two sweaters from Sunrise Clothing Store, 123 Main Street, Clinton, Iowa 51030. The catalog order number is SW056. Use block style.

Combining Good and Bad News

Activity E

Chapter 5

Name_____

Date_____ Period_____

Imagine you work for Sunrise Clothing Store, a mail order business. Prepare a bad-news letter in response to the following letter. Enter your letter into a word processing document. Use modified block style. Be sure to include each of the eight standard parts of the business letter. In the box below, prepare an envelope for your letter with a return address.

Route 1
Clinton, Iowa 51030
February 22, 20xx

Manager
Sunrise Clothing Store
123 Main Street
Clinton, Iowa 51303

Dear Sir or Madam:

I recently bought two sweaters from your store. After washing one sweater, it shrank. Now the sweater is too small, and I can't wear it. It also changed color. I would like to return both sweaters and get my money back. Should I mail both of them to you?

Sincerely,

Martha Greenwell

Martha Greenwell

Writing Memos

Name_____

Date_____Period_____

Imagine you are a supervisor at the King Manufacturing Company. As a supervisor, you must inform the workers in your section about a meeting that is to take place next Wednesday at 10:00 a.m. The purpose of the meeting is to explain new safety policies to all employees. The meeting will be held in the company's lunchroom where coffee, soft drinks, and doughnuts will be served. Using the form below, prepare a memo to the employees in your section.

King Manufacturing Company

MEMO

DATE:

TO:

FROM:

SUBJECT:

Telephone Skills

Activity G

Chapter 5

Name_____

Date_____Period_____

Work with a partner to role-play the following situation. Have your partner imagine calling the law firm of Entis, Entis, and Martinez to arrange an interview for a school project. Role-play the part of the receptionist and ask if you can take a message for Ms. Entis, who is not available to take the call. Use the form below to take the message, then switch roles with your partner and repeat the role-play. Evaluate your partner's telephone skills by answering the questions below.

To _____

Date _____ Time_____

TELEPHONE MESSAGE/WHILE YOU WERE OUT

M_____

of _____

Phone _____

☐ Telephoned   ☐ Will call again

☐ Returned your call   ☐ Called to see you

☐ Please call   ☐ Wants to see you

Message _____

_____

_____

_____

_____

_____

_____

Message taken by _____

1. Was the call answered immediately? _____

2. Was the caller greeted pleasantly?_____

3. Was the voice clear and distinct?_____

4. Was proper grammar used? _____

5. Was the message read back to the caller?_____

6. Did the message contain all the key facts?_____

Your Speaking Skills

Activity H   Name_____

Chapter 5   Date_____Period_____

Imagine you are a school news reporter on special assignment for a local television station. Your assignment is to prepare a 90-second news report entitled "Work-Based Learning at (Your School)." Plan your report to cover the most important facts. (You may wish to report on class assignments, class activities, and jobs.) On another sheet of paper, write a brief outline of your report.

Present your report to the class, making sure it is 90-seconds long. (If possible, have your report video recorded or audiotaped.) Ask class members to evaluate you according to the six areas listed below. Then answer the following questions by summarizing their evaluations and evaluating yourself.

1. Speaking rate: _____

   _____

2. Eye contact: _____

   _____

3. Proper use of English: _____

   _____

4. Clear and distinct speech:_____

   _____

5. Nonverbal communication: _____

   _____

6. Other comments: _____

   _____

Based on the evaluations given by class members, how would you rate yourself as a speaker?_____

_____

_____

_____

What are your weaknesses as a speaker?_____

_____

_____

_____

How can you improve as a speaker? _____

_____

_____

_____

What are your strengths as a speaker? _____

_____

 **Math in the Workplace**

Making Change

Name_____

Date_____Period_____

1. Suppose you work in a grocery store and a customer gives you a $20 bill for a $5.47 purchase. The total amount of change you should hand back is $_____. In the space provided below, write what you would say as you make change for the customer.

_____

_____

_____

_____

_____

_____

_____

_____

_____

_____

_____

_____

_____

2. Work with a partner to calculate the amount of change for each of the transactions below. Then practice counting back the change to each other.

Purchase Price	Amount Tendered	Change
$ 4.23	Ten-dollar bill	_____
$10.34	A ten and a five-dollar bill	_____
$ 1.55	Five-dollar bill	_____
$11.75	Twenty-dollar bill	_____
$ 2.16	Three one-dollar bills	_____
$ 7.45	Fifty-dollar bill	_____

Using a Calculator

Activity B

Chapter 6

Name_____

Date_____ Period_____

Use a calculator to solve these math problems. If necessary, review the procedure in the text describing how to operate a calculator. Round off answers to the nearest hundredths.

Addition:

1. 75
    69
    + 34

2. 204
    389
    + 756

3. 248.70
    684.38
    + 193.95

4. 1,643.50
    2,978.32
    + 4,859.18

Subtraction:

5. 196
    − 28

6. 2,487
    − 1,598

7. 1,369.00
    − 951.83

8. 16,874
    − 13,928

Multiplication:

9. 603
    × 86

10. 1,936
    × 367

11. 769
    × .29

12. 14,792
    × 49

Division:

13. 1,204 ÷ 28 = _____

14. 15,675 ÷ 57 = _____

15. 2,878.40 ÷ 67 = _____

16. 45,938 ÷ 340 = _____

Fractions, Decimals, and Percentages

Activity C

Chapter 6

Name_____

Date_____ Period_____

Write the way you would read the common fractions below.

1. 4/10_____

2. 5/16_____

3. 18/27_____

4. 11/22 _____

5. 3/5 _____

6. 125/300 _____

Write the way you would read the decimal fractions below.

7. 0.075 _____

8. 0.95 _____

9. 0.6 _____

10. 0.5621 _____

11. 0.55_____

12. 0.9_____

13. 0.0088_____

14. 0.634_____

Change the following fractions into decimals. Round off to the nearest hundredth.

15. 25/75_____

16. 4/5 _____

17. 7/4_____

18. 125/100 _____

19. 11/22 _____

20. 16/64 _____

Calculate the answer for the following problems. Round off to the nearest hundredth.

21. If the sales tax rate in your state is 6½%, what is the tax on your purchase of shoes costing $22.99?_____

_____

22. If the profit on a car priced at $12,350 is 15%, how much will the seller make?_____

_____

23. If the discount on a computer costing $1,500 is 25%, what is the amount of the discount? _____

_____

24. If the unemployment rate in your state is 3½% and there are 2,500,000 employable people in your state, how many people are unemployed? _____

_____

Taking Measurements

Activity D
Chapter 6

Name_____

Date_____ Period_____

Using a ruler, draw lines of the following lengths:

1. ¾ inch

2. 3 inches

3. 1¼ inches

4. 2⅜ inches

5. 3½ inches

Measure length and width of this card:

6. Length:_____ Width:_____

Use a ruler or tape measure to measure the following items:

	Length	Width	Height (or thickness)
7. Workbook for *From School to Work*	_____	_____	_____
8. The dimensions of your classroom	_____	_____	_____
9. The door of your classroom	_____	_____	_____
10. The classroom's board	_____	_____	_____
11. One-dollar bill (U.S.)	_____	_____	_____

Find the area of the geometric shapes shown below.

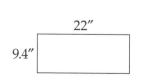
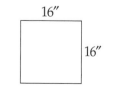

12._____   13. _____   14. _____   15. _____

Working with Metrics

Activity E

Chapter 6

Name_____

Date_____Period_____

Answer the following questions using the metric conversion chart in the text on page 133.

_____ 1. Tanisha drank 12 ounces of milk. How many milliliters of milk did she drink?

_____ 2. The speed limit is 65 miles per hour. What is the speed limit in kilometers per hour?

_____ 3. The length of a football field is 100 yards. What is the length in meters?

_____ 4. Sue weighs 110 pounds. What is her weight in kilograms?

_____ 5. Manuel bought 40 liters of gasoline. How many gallons did he buy?

_____ 6. The temperature is 30 degrees Celsius. What is the temperature in degrees Fahrenheit?

_____ 7. Ira bought a picture frame that is 8×10 inches. What is the size of the frame in centimeters?

_____ 8. Cindy needs 5½ yards of fabric to cover a chair. How many meters of fabric does she need?

_____ 9. Lei's body temperature is 100 degrees Fahrenheit. What is her temperature in degrees Celsius?

_____ 10. The distance from Tampa to Miami is 300 kilometers. What is the distance in miles?

_____ 11. The width of Jeff's room is 400 centimeters. How wide is the room in inches?

_____ 12. Chun bought a steak weighing 344 grams. How many ounces does the steak weigh?

_____ 13. Sara bought a quart of orange juice. How many liters of orange juice did she buy?

_____ 14. The length of a swimming pool is 12 meters. What is the length in feet?

Analyzing Data

Name_____

Date_____Period_____

Analyze the chart to answer the first four questions. Then match the following chapter terms with their descriptions by writing the correct letter in each blank.

Atlantic Accounting Company		
Salary	**Number of Employees**	**Salary × Number**
$75,000	2 (5+ yrs. of service)	$150,000
$60,000	3 (2-5 yrs. of service)	$180,000
$42,000	4 (2-15 mos. of service)	$168,000
Total	9	$498,000

1. What is the mean salary? _____

2. What is the mode of the salaries? _____

3. What is the median of the salaries?_____

4. To a job applicant, which average is of greatest importance? _____

_____

Description

_____ 5. A fraction with a denominator (or multiple) of 10.

_____ 6. Arranges data in rows and columns.

_____ 7. Shows the relationship of two or more variables.

_____ 8. Shows comparisons between categories.

_____ 9. Shows the relationship of parts to the whole.

_____ 10. Presents information with the use of eye-catching images.

Chart Name

A. bar graph

B. circle graph

C. common fraction

D. decimal fraction

E. line graph

F. pictograph

G. table

Technology and You

Computer Hardware

Name_____

Date_____ Period_____

Complete the following statements by filling in the blanks.

_____ 1. A lightweight, portable computer the size of a notebook is a _____.

_____ 2. The physical equipment used in computer systems is the _____.

_____ 3. The central processing unit (CPU), also called the _____, controls what is done with the data received by the computer.

_____ 4. The amount of _____ _____ Memory on a computer affects how quickly it processes and runs programs.

_____ 5. A video card helps the computer process complex _____, such as those found on the Internet and in games.

_____ 6. The internal _____ _____ drive of a computer stores the data to operate the computer, as well as all information entered by the user.

_____ 7. Writable CDs, DVDs and USB flash drives are all examples of _____ devices.

_____ 8. Multiple computer terminals that can share information are linked through a closed _____.

_____ 9. A _____ is a computer with extensive memory that is connected to other computers and allows businesses to regularly back up information.

_____ 10. Keeping your files organized and easily retrievable on the computer is accomplished by using good file_____.

_____ 11. _____ are any output and input devices that are plugged into a computer's CPU.

_____ 12. A device that passes an electron beam over an image, allowing the image to be stored in the computer's memory, is called a _____.

_____ 13. Photos taken by a digital camera are saved on _____ _____ cards instead of film.

_____ 14. Keyboards, mice, scanners, digital cameras, and webcams are all examples of _____ devices.

_____ 15. Monitors and printers are examples of _____ devices.

_____ 16. Cameras that are plugged into a computer and used to transmit videos to the Internet are called _____.

Investigating Web Sites

Activity B   Name_____

Chapter 7   Date _____Period_____

Web sites are maintained by educational institutions, companies, organizations, government agencies, and individuals. It is important to be able to evaluate Web sites for credibility, accuracy, and timely information. Use a search engine to gather information about the key word *copyright*. Choose one Web address returned and evaluate the site using the following questions. Compare your findings with classmates.

Search engine used: _____

URL of the Web site: _____

Who created the Web site?

What does the domain extension of the page (.gov, .edu, .com, .org) tell about the site?

When was the Web site last updated?

Where do links from this Web site take you?

How do you know this Web site is credible?
- Is the content accurate and objective?

- Is a bibliography of sources included?

- Is contact information available?

- Are the spelling and grammar correct?

- Does the information appear biased?

- Do pictures, photographs, and graphics add to the information?

List several key points of information you discovered about copyrights from this Web site:

✓

✓

✓

Essential Technology Skills Self-Check

Activity C

Chapter 7

Name _____

Date _____ Period _____

Being familiar with computer technology is crucial for job success. Reflect on your skills for using technology by completing the self-assessment.

Computer Hardware Skills	Have	Need
1. Identify parts of a computer system including CPU, keyboard, monitor, mouse, speakers, printer, ports, and CD-ROM drive		
2. Set up new computer, connecting peripheral equipment		
3. Adjust display settings		
4. Insert, access, and eject a CD and/or USB flash drive		
5. Install new software and application		
6. Add memory to central processing unit (CPU)		
7. Transfer pictures/video from a digital camera or other media devices		
8. Scan a document and store as a file		
9. Determine available space on a drive/file/directory		
10. Troubleshoot problems, including memory and program compatibility		
11. Install/maintain virus protection and check for viruses		
12. Select and use printer; cancel print jobs		
General Computer Skills	**Have**	**Need**
13. Open programs and files		
14. Access help menus		
15. Navigate the desktop		
16. Resize and move windows and objects to new locations		
17. Navigate documents and dialog boxes by using vertical and horizontal scroll bars, mouse, directional arrows, and shortcut keys		
18. Customize menu and toolbars		
19. File management (locate, rename, and delete files, folders, and icons)		
20. Use directory structures to organize documents		
Computer Software Skills	**Have**	**Need**
21. Create, save, and print a word processing document		
22. Format text		
23. Edit by deleting, adding, and replacing characters and sections of text		
24. Cut/copy/paste text and objects into new locations		
25. Use of tool bars, spell check, print preview, search, and replace		
26. Draw a simple illustration using draw toolbars		
27. Create a spreadsheet using mathematical formulas and functions		
28. Import files into spreadsheets, databases, and/or word processing documents		
29. Sort data in a table and/or spreadsheet		
30. Create a database to store and retrieve records		
31. Create, edit, and produce a brochure or newsletter		
32. Create an electronic presentation/slide show		
Internet and E-Mail Skills	**Have**	**Need**
33. Connect to the Internet using a service provider		
34. Access a Web page by entering a URL, using a bookmark, or following a link		
35. Conduct Web searches using search engines		
36. Compose, address, and send e-mail		
37. Reply to and forward e-mail		
38. Add, open, and save attachments		
39. Print messages and attachments		
40. Create distribution lists		

The Impact of Technology

Activity D   Name _____

Chapter 7   Date _____ Period _____

Computers play an important part on the job, at school and in the home. List three ways computers are used in each area below. Then answer the questions that follow.

Technology on the job:

1. _____

_____

2. _____

_____

3. _____

_____

Technology at school:

1. _____

_____

2. _____

_____

3. _____

_____

Technology in the home:

1. _____

_____

2. _____

_____

3. _____

_____

A. What types of technology have you used this past week?_____

_____

_____

_____

_____

(Continued)

Name_____

B. How is technology used in your present job or at school?_____

_____

_____

_____

C. What technology courses have you taken (keyboarding, software applications, desktop publishing, computer-aided drafting, programming, multimedia, etc.)?_____

_____

_____

_____

D. What technology skills will be needed for employment in the future?_____

_____

_____

_____

E. How will technology affect the way you live and work in the next five years? _____

_____

Next ten years? _____

_____

Next twenty years? _____

_____

F. What emerging technology do you think will be in every automobile within the next five years?

_____

_____

_____

Computer-Related Careers

Activity E   Name _____

Chapter 7   Date _____ Period _____

Match the following occupations to the appropriate job descriptions by writing the correct letter in each blank. Then answer the questions below.

_____ 1. Writes a program to set up a payroll system.

_____ 2. Repairs computer equipment.

_____ 3. Links a company's manufacturing operations to automatic inventory control.

_____ 4. Codes instructions for the tools used to cut metal sections for automobile parts.

_____ 5. Performs routine computer operations in an office.

_____ 6. Inputs data into a computer system.

_____ 7. Creates and maintains a company's Web site.

A. computer operator
B. computer service technician
C. computer systems analyst
D. data entry keyer
E. software developer
F. tool programmer
G. Webmaster

8. Think of an occupation you might like to have in the future. Which technology applications would you use in that occupation? _____

_____

_____

_____

_____

_____

_____

9. Where would you receive training to operate the technology? _____

_____

_____

_____

_____

10. What jobs will be changed with the advancement of technology? _____

_____

_____

_____

_____

 **Looking Good on the Job**

MyPyramid Plan

| Activity A | Name_____ |
| Chapter 8 | Date_____ Period_____ |

Log on to the www.MyPyramid.gov Web site. Click on the subject *MyPyramid Plan*. Enter your age, gender, and physical activity to generate your personal MyPyramid plan. Print the PDF version of your results and use it to complete the chart below.

Food Group	Recommended Amount
Grains	
Vegetables	
Fruits	
Milk	
Meat and beans	
Total calories	
Physical activity (minutes)	

Using foods and beverages typically available to you, plan a one-day menu that follows your personalized plan, including snacks. Use the Web site as a resource to help you determine the ounce-equivalents for grains and meat and beans.

Breakfast menu:

_____

_____

_____

_____

Lunch menu:

_____

_____

_____

_____

Dinner menu:

_____

_____

_____

Snacks menu:

_____

_____

_____

(Continued)

Name_____

1. Did you eat the recommended servings from each food group? Explain. _____

   _____

   _____

   _____

   _____

   _____

   _____

2. How do the number and types of meals you eat every day affect how you feel? _____

   _____

   _____

   _____

3. Why is it necessary to include sources from each food group in your daily diet? _____

   _____

   _____

4. Did you eat a variety of foods this day? Explain why or why not._____

   _____

   _____

   _____

5. Of the foods you ate, which provided starch? _____

   _____

6. Of the foods you ate, which provided fiber? _____

   _____

7. Did you limit your intake of foods containing fats, sugar, and sodium? _____

8. What steps can you take to improve your eating habits?_____

   _____

   _____

   _____

   _____

   _____

Exercise Regularly

Activity B
Chapter 8

Name_____

Date_____ Period_____

The chart below shows a good fitness plan for Jamie, a healthy teen of average height and weight. Using the information in the chart, answer the questions in the spaces provided.

Jamie's Fitness Plan

Type: Aerobic dancing
Place: Physical education class and aerobic dance classes
Time of day: During and after school
Duration: 40 minutes
Frequency: 5 times a week
Warm-up exercises: 5 minutes of leg stretches, toe touches, and limbering up body by slowly running in place to gradually increase heart circulation
Cool-down exercises: 5 minutes of slow running in place, then stress-reduction relaxation

---

1. How can Jamie benefit from exercising regularly? _____

   _____

2. Why did Jamie incorporate warm-up and cool-down exercises into her fitness program? _____

   _____

3. What exercises does Jamie do to develop her muscle strength, coordination, and flexibility? _____

   _____

4. Jamie chose aerobic dancing because she enjoys it. What other activities could Jamie do to exercise the heart and lungs?_____

   _____

5. In the space below, make a fitness plan like Jamie's for yourself.

   Type of activity: _____

   Place of activity: _____

   Time of day:_____

   Activity duration:_____

   Activity frequency: _____

   Warm-up exercises: _____

   _____

   _____

   Cool-down exercises:_____

   _____

   _____

Looking Good

Activity C   Name_____

Chapter 8   Date_____ Period_____

Read the story about Ron. Then fill in the blanks to complete the following grooming tips that could help Ron improve his appearance.

Ron's Appearance

Ron seems to be a nice person, but people usually try to avoid him. He is not very clean, and his clothes never seem to look right on him. Ron probably was never taught to take care of his hair, clothes, and body. As a result, Ron does not look good on the job or at school.

---

1. Good _____ is essential to getting and keeping a job.

2. Keeping the body clean is called good _____ .

3. Use a(n) _____ or _____ to help control body odor.

4. For the clean-shaven look, most men must _____ every day.

5. To maintain a beard or mustache, it should be neatly combed and _____ .

6. Shaving under the arms can help reduce _____ odor.

7. To keep the skin free of bacteria, dirt, and oils, a person should _____ regularly with warm soapy water or a cleanser.

8. For problem skin, the person to see for help is a(n) _____ .

9. Since your hair can greatly enhance your personal appearance, it is important to keep your hair

   _____ and _____ .

10. A(n) _____ will be able to help you choose the best hair style for you.

11. Keep hands and fingernails clean and neatly _____ .

12. For clean, healthy teeth and fresh breath, a person should _____ their teeth regularly.

13. A person is dressed right for the job if he or she wears clean clothes that fit properly and are

    _____ for the workplace.

14. A good way to decide what is best to wear to work is to know your company's _____

    _____ .

15. Caring for your clothes by keeping them clean, neatly pressed, and mended will help you have a(n)

    _____ _____ .

Appropriate Clothes for the Job

Activity D   Name_____

Chapter 8   Date_____Period_____

Answer the following questions about what clothes are appropriate for various types of jobs, including your job. Then discuss your answers with the class.

1. What clothes would be most appropriate if you worked

   A. in a bakery? _____

   _____

   B. as a construction worker? _____

   _____

   C. in a child care center? _____

   _____

   D. as a receptionist in an office? _____

   _____

   E. as a clerk in a grocery store?_____

   _____

   F. as an auto mechanic? _____

   _____

   G. as a computer analyst?_____

   _____

   H. as a medical technician? _____

   _____

   _____

   I. as a landscaper? _____

   _____

   J. as a salesperson in a department store? _____

   _____

2. Name another job and describe the type of clothes appropriate for it.

   Job: _____

   Appropriate clothes: _____

   _____

3. Describe the type of clothes appropriate to wear to your workplace.

   Job: _____

   Appropriate clothes: _____

   _____

Your Wardrobe

Activity E	Name_____
Chapter 8	Date_____Period_____

Evaluate your wardrobe by following the steps below.

1. On a separate sheet of paper, prepare a wardrobe inventory. List all the clothes, shoes, and accessories you have for school, work, and other occasions. As you examine each item, decide whether you will keep (K), discard (D), or replace (R) it. Put the appropriate letter next to each item on your list.

2. Using your inventory, identify the gaps in your wardrobe. Review the items you want to replace and list them in the following chart. Then add the new items you want. Estimate the costs of new purchases, using information found on the Internet or a catalog for reference if necessary.

Wardrobe Planning		
Wardrobe Gaps	**Items Needed**	**Cost Estimates**
		Total

3. Describe how to care for your clothes properly. _____

_____

_____

4. Identify factors important to dressing appropriately for the workplace._____

_____

_____

# Safety on the Job

Job Safety Procedures

Activity A

Chapter 9

Name_____

Date_____ Period_____

Interview a supervisor who is responsible for job safety procedures. Consult the employee handbook and answer the following questions.

1. Is your work site safe at all times? Explain. _____

_____

_____

2. How do you maintain a safety-conscious attitude at all times? Explain. _____

_____

_____

3. What safety rules and regulations must you follow?_____

_____

_____

4. What safety signs are posted at your work site? _____

_____

5. What does your employee handbook say about safety?_____

_____

6. What type of fire extinguisher is available?_____

_____

_____

7. Where at your work site are the following located: fire extinguisher? fire alarm? emergency exits?_____

_____

_____

8. Where are emergency phone numbers posted?_____

_____

9. Are there pieces of equipment at your work site that some employees cannot legally operate because of age? Explain. _____

_____

Protection from Environmental Hazards

Activity B   Name _____

Chapter 9   Date _____ Period _____

Match the environmental hazards with the proper protective clothing or device.

_____ 1. High frequency sounds.

_____ 2. Eye injuries.

_____ 3. Welding burns.

_____ 4. Harmful gases.

_____ 5. Burns from flames and hot metal.

_____ 6. Burns from acids, caustics, and alkalies.

_____ 7. Cuts and abrasions on the hands.

_____ 8. Injuries from falling objects.

A. asbestos gloves and leggings

B. masks and respirators

C. rubber gloves, aprons, and face shields

D. hard hats and safety shoes

E. gloves

F. leather gloves and apron shields

G. earplugs and earmuffs

H. safety goggles and face shields

Describe the environmental hazards (if any) that you might encounter on your job or at school. _____

_____

_____

_____

How can you protect yourself from these environmental hazards? _____

_____

_____

_____

_____

What training in universal precautions should all workers receive? _____

_____

_____

_____

List the basic first aid steps to follow when a person is injured in an accident. _____

_____

_____

_____

_____

Accident Prevention

Activity C

Chapter 9

Name _____

Date _____ Period _____

Answer the following questions regarding safety at your workplace.

Your type of work: _____

_____

Describe an accident that has occurred on the job, either to you or to someone else. _____

_____

_____

_____

_____

Explain how the accident could have been prevented. _____

_____

_____

_____

_____

What safety procedures can you follow on the job to help prevent accidents? _____

_____

_____

_____

What does your employer do to make the workplace safe?_____

_____

_____

What type of safety training have you had on your present or former jobs?_____

_____

_____

Why is it to your employer's advantage to promote safety at the workplace? _____

_____

_____

_____

Workplace Violence Awareness

Activity D   Name_____

Chapter 9   Date_____ Period_____

For each statement below, circle *T* if it is true or *F* if it is false.

T   F   1. Workplace violence is not a serious problem in America.

T   F   2. Workplace violence is always a physical attack.

T   F   3. Customers sometimes commit violence in the workplace.

T   F   4. Robbery can be a motive for violence in the workplace.

T   F   5. Workplace violence includes threatening behavior.

T   F   6. A mentally unstable person may commit workplace violence because of an imagined problem.

T   F   7. Pushing someone is not a physical act of violence.

T   F   8. Swearing is a form of workplace violence.

T   F   9. There is no need to alert your supervisor if you have safety concerns.

T   F   10. A person who works alone has a greater chance of being a victim of workplace violence.

T   F   11. Domestic problems can be a motive to commit workplace violence.

T   F   12. Most murders in the workplace are connected to a robbery.

T   F   13. Where you work is not an important factor in workplace violence.

T   F   14. Retail businesses are less prone to workplace violence.

T   F   15. Installing surveillance systems may help prevent workplace violence.

T   F   16. A written threat is a psychological attack.

T   F   17. Harassment is a form of psychological violence.

T   F   18. Learning how to recognize potentially violent situations will not help prevent workplace violence.

Safety Committee Presentation

Activity E

Chapter 9

Name_____

Date_____Period_____

Imagine you are a member of a safety committee. Working with two or three classmates, choose one of the topics listed below and develop the topic into a presentation on workplace safety useful for staff training. Research current facts on the topic and learn about the latest technology and recommended procedures related to it. Make a group presentation to the class, reporting your findings and demonstrating any key procedures. Briefly outline your group's presentation below.

Choice of topics:

1. Fire and weather-warning safety, types and proper use of fire extinguishers, and evacuation procedures

2. Health safety, including first aid and universal precautions

3. Office safety, including ergonomics and air quality

4. Food service safety, including food handling procedures and proper use of machinery, cleaning agents, and protective clothing

5. Road-related safety, including vehicle maintenance and driver training and testing requirements

Presentation outline:

_____

_____

_____

_____

_____

_____

_____

_____

_____

_____

_____

_____

_____

_____

_____

_____

_____

_____

_____

Protective Devices and Procedures

Activity F

Chapter 9

Name_____

Date_____Period_____

For the occupations identified at the top of the chart, check the appropriate protective devices and procedures you would recommend to help workers avoid accidents on their jobs.

	Firefighter	Geologist	Welder	Airline Pilot	Surgeon	Salesclerk	Dental hygienist	Programmer	Auto technician	Coal miner	Your job
Devices:											
Leather gloves and apron											
Gloves											
Safety goggles and face shields											
Hard hats and safety shoes											
Rubber gloves, aprons, face shields											
Earplugs and earmuffs											
Mask and respirator											
Procedures:											
Conduct fire drills.											
Conduct random drug tests.											
Label and handle chemicals properly.											
Read OSHA poster at worksite.											
Report all job injuries.											

Leadership and Group Dynamics

What Makes a Leader?

Activity A	Name_____
Chapter 10	Date_____Period_____

Think about leaders you have known at school and on the job. From your experience, which leadership skills do you feel are the most important? Rate the following leadership skills and qualities in order of importance to you from 1 (most important) to 15 (least important). Then work with a small group of classmates to determine the top five choices of your group. Report your group's findings to the class.

_____ Has the ability to motivate team members to support a vision and achieve goals.

_____ Assumes responsibility for the duties of the office or position.

_____ Always shows confidence.

_____ Keeps the team focused.

_____ Analyzes situations clearly and takes decisive action when needed.

_____ Takes risks and explores new ways of achieving goals.

_____ Encourages team spirit and cooperation among members.

_____ Listens to others and responds to their views.

_____ Delegates assignments fairly.

_____ Recognizes the accomplishments of others.

_____ Welcomes new ideas.

_____ Sets a good example for members.

_____ Works for group, not personal, success.

_____ Does a fair share of work.

_____ Stays up-to-date on important issues.

What other skills or abilities do you feel a leader should possess?

_____

_____

_____

_____

_____

_____

Evaluating Leaders

Name_____

Date_____Period_____

Read the following list of leadership qualities. If the leadership quality is a positive quality, write *P* in the blank. Write *N* in the blank if the leadership quality is negative. Then in the chart below, name local or national leaders that impress you and explain why.

_____ 1. Sets goals that have been expressed by the group.

_____ 2. Is able to delegate responsibility.

_____ 3. Appoints only friends to committees.

_____ 4. Does not listen to the opinions of others.

_____ 5. Gives credit to others for the work they do.

_____ 6. Challenges and encourages others to action.

_____ 7. Works for group success.

_____ 8. Works only for personal success.

_____ 9. Assumes the responsibility for the duties of the office.

_____ 10. Analyzes situations clearly and will take decisive action when needed.

_____ 11. Shows confidence in ability to lead a group.

_____ 12. Is enthusiastic.

_____ 13. Cannot motivate the group.

_____ 14. Has a vision that is important to the organization.

_____ 15. Gets others to do all the work.

Impressive Leaders	
Name of Leader:	**Key Quality or Ability**

Leadership and Group Dynamics

Activity C

Chapter 10

Name_____

Date_____Period_____

Read the case studies below to determine the types of leadership and group dynamics illustrated in each. Explain the reason for your decisions by answering the questions that follow.

Case 1. At a staff meeting, Robin mentioned that a social activity planned for Friday interfered with the religious holiday of some employees. It was brought to her attention right before the meeting. Robin has always tried to be fair and courteous to coworkers from other cultures. Consequently, all her coworkers listen to her and value her comments. Robin asked for discussion on rescheduling the event and her coworkers agreed. They felt everyone would benefit if the social event were held on an alternative date.

What type of leadership did Robin demonstrate? Explain._____

_____

_____

_____

_____

What group dynamics were evident at the meeting?_____

_____

_____

_____

_____

Case 2. There was an opening posted for a team leader on the evening shift at the music store where Tyrone and Doug work. Both Tyrone and Doug applied for the position. The new store manager had not worked with the staff very long. He selected Tyrone as team leader because Tyrone had worked there longer. As the new team leader, Tyrone immediately made changes in work schedules that gave his best friend, Cliff, Friday and Saturday evenings off. Tyrone also assigned Doug the undesirable task of restocking store items. Team members were unhappy that weekend shifts and job tasks were no longer rotated.

What type of leadership did Tyrone demonstrate? Explain._____

_____

_____

_____

_____

What group dynamics are likely to occur because of the new team leader's decisions? _____

_____

_____

_____

_____

Career and Technical Student Organizations

Activity D   Name_____

Chapter 10   Date_____Period_____

Working with two or three classmates, research career and technical student organizations (CTSOs). Use the letter clues to determine formal names. You may want to interview members of the organization at your school or access the Web sites noted in the chapter to gather facts. Use the information to complete the chart below. If you have a CTSO at your school that is not listed, add it to the chart.

CTSO Clues	Formal Name	Target Membership	Mission or Goal	At your school?
BPA				
DECA				
FBLA				
FCCLA				
FFA				
HOSA				
SKILLS				
TSA				
Other:				

Leadership Self-Evaluation

Activity E

Chapter 10

Name_____

Date_____Period_____

Evaluate your leadership skills by placing a check in the appropriate spaces. Then answer the questions that follow.

Leadership Skills					
How do I perform in these areas?	**Very Good**	**Good**	**Fair**	**Poor**	**Do Not Possess**
Work well with others.					
Delegate tasks fairly.					
Encourage team spirit.					
Know what is important to an organization.					
Demonstrate honesty and truthfulness.					
Use imagination and creative skills.					
Teach others new skills and knowledge.					
Help others recognize their abilities.					
Communicate clearly.					
Know and use parliamentary procedure.					
Motivate team members into action.					
Listen carefully to others.					
Use decision-making skills well.					
Set a good example.					
Keep up-to-date on new skills or ideas.					
Take responsibility for team decisions or actions.					
Work for group, not personal, success.					
Manage group conflict.					
Negotiate agreements between opposing views.					
Deal with dissatisfied "customers."					

(Continued)

Name_____

1. What other skills do you possess that will help you become a better leader? _____

_____

_____

2. What activities and groups do you belong to that increase your skills in leadership? _____

_____

_____

3. What new activities or groups might you join to strengthen your leadership skills? _____

_____

_____

4. What are some qualities of poor leadership? _____

_____

_____

5. How does poor leadership affect a group's performance? _____

_____

_____

6. Give examples of occasions when you were a leader. _____

_____

_____

7. What frustrations have you encountered as a leader? _____

_____

_____

8. If you could give advice to a new leader at work or in a group at school, what would you say? _____

_____

_____

Participating in Meetings

Terms Used at Meetings

Activity A

Chapter 11

Name_____

Date_____Period_____

The following terms are often used in meetings. Match each term with its description by writing the correct letter in the blank.

_____ 1. To end a meeting.

_____ 2. A list of things to be done and discussed at a meeting.

_____ 3. To change the wording of a motion that has been made.

_____ 4. The presiding officer at a meeting, such as the president or chairperson.

_____ 5. To speak for or against a motion.

_____ 6. At least one more than half of the members present at the meeting.

_____ 7. A written record of the business covered at a meeting.

_____ 8. The rules and regulations that govern the organization.

_____ 9. An orderly way of conducting a business meeting that helps groups conduct meetings in an efficient and fair manner.

_____ 10. A recommendation by a member that certain action is taken by the group.

_____ 11. The number of members who must be present to legally conduct business at a meeting.

_____ 12. The approval of a motion by another member.

_____ 13. To delay making a decision on a motion.

_____ 14. The right to speak in a meeting without interruption from others.

_____ 15. The formal term for *yes*.

_____ 16. Permanent committees of the group.

A. adjourn

B. agenda

C. amend the motion

D. aye

E. bylaws

F. chair

G. debate

H. majority

I. minutes

J. motion

K. nay

L. parliamentary procedure

M. quorum

N. second the motion

O. standing committees

P. table the motion

Q. the floor

Order of Business

Activity B

Chapter 11

Name_____

Date_____ Period_____

Unscramble the order of business for a meeting by numbering the following parts of a meeting according to the parliamentary procedure discussed in the text. Then answer the questions below.

_____ Marsha, chairperson of the banquet committee, gives her report.

_____ A motion to hold a bake sale, which was tabled from the last meeting, is discussed.

_____ Jim announces that the paper drive will continue for another week and group members should bring papers in on Friday.

_____ Jane, the president, calls the meeting to order.

_____ Maria, the program chairperson, introduces the guest speaker.

_____ After a motion and a second motion, Jane declares the meeting adjourned.

_____ Bill, the secretary, reads the minutes of the previous meeting.

_____ An idea for a group picnic is brought up.

_____ Jerry, the treasurer, gives his report.

_____ Juan, chairperson of the membership committee, gives his report.

What is the purpose of using parliamentary procedure to conduct a meeting?

_____

_____

_____

_____

_____

_____

_____

_____

What items are on a typical meeting agenda from your group?

_____

_____

_____

_____

_____

_____

_____

_____

_____

Organization Constitutions and Bylaws

Activity C

Chapter 11

Name_____

Date_____Period_____

Obtain and read a copy of the constitution and bylaws of a school organization you belong to or might like to join. Then answer the following questions and report your findings to the class.

1. What is the purpose of the organization? _____

_____

_____

_____

_____

_____

_____

_____

_____

2. What is the order of business that is followed by this organization? _____

_____

_____

_____

_____

_____

_____

_____

_____

_____

3. Does this organization base its meetings on parliamentary procedure? Explain._____

_____

_____

_____

_____

_____

_____

(Continued)

Name_____

4. According to the constitution and bylaws, what is a quorum?_____

_____

_____

_____

5. What are the organization's standing committees? _____

_____

_____

_____

_____

_____

_____

6. How are officers nominated and elected? _____

_____

_____

_____

_____

_____

_____

_____

7. How are committee chairpersons selected?_____

_____

_____

_____

_____

8. How are motions handled?_____

_____

_____

_____

_____

Conducting a Meeting

Activity D

Chapter 11

Name_____

Date_____Period_____

Work in small groups to participate in a class-wide mock meeting that uses the rules of parliamentary procedure. With two or three classmates, prepare one of the orders of business listed below. (Your teacher may make group assignments.) Then, at the appropriate time, present your group's portion of the meeting. After the meeting, answer the questions that follow.

Call to Order

Select a person to act as president of the group. Then, as a group, prepare an agenda following *Robert's Rules of Order* and discuss what the president will do during the meeting. The president will conduct the meeting following the agenda your group prepares.

Reading and Approving of Minutes

Select a person to act as secretary. As a group, prepare minutes from your last meeting, which the secretary will read during the mock meeting. Also discuss what the secretary will do during the meeting. Select another member of the group to take minutes of the current meeting.

Reports of Officers

Select a person to act as treasurer. Prepare a treasurer's report using the following information: beginning balance—$120; money collected from dues—$345; refreshments for the last meeting—$30; state dues paid—$300. Then discuss what the treasurer will do during the meeting.

Standing Committee Reports

Select a chairperson for this committee. Prepare a report on refreshments for the next meeting. What refreshments will you have? How much money will be needed? Who will purchase the refreshments? Who will set up the refreshments and clean up after the meeting? How much money must each member contribute? When is the money due?

Special Committee

Select a chairperson for this committee. Prepare a report on all aspects of painting a poster for homecoming. Who will secure a site for hanging the poster? What materials will you need? Who will get the materials? What is the theme? When will you paint the poster? Who will clean up?

Unfinished Business

Select a chairperson for this committee. The chairperson will announce that a motion to have a fund-raiser was tabled at the last meeting. Discuss the advantages or disadvantages of selling candy in school.

New Business, Announcements, and Adjournment

Select a chairperson for this committee. The chairperson will announce that a date for the next meeting should be set. You will also make an announcement about the district elections, which will be held on October 1 at the Town City Center on Main Street. Be sure to discuss the attire for the day, which is business dress. This group should also move for adjournment at the appropriate time.

1. Was a quorum present?_____

2. What number of people represented a quorum?_____

3. Did the president prepare and follow an agenda based on *Robert's Rules of Order*?_____

4. Did the president ask for corrections or additions to the minutes? _____

(Continued)

Name_____

5. Was the treasurer's report accurate? _____

6. Did the standing committee include all necessary information in its report? _____

7. Did the special committee include all necessary information in its report?_____

8. Did the committee for unfinished business lead the discussion on the candy sale?_____

9. Did the committee for new business achieve its purpose? _____

10. Did the announcement contain complete information?_____

11. Was the motion to adjourn stated properly? _____

12. What did you learn from the mock meeting that can be applied to real meetings you attend in the future?

_____

_____

_____

_____

_____

_____

_____

_____

_____

_____

_____

_____

_____

_____

_____

_____

_____

_____

_____

_____

_____

_____

_____

_____

12 Learning About Yourself

How I See Myself

Name_____

Date_____Period_____

Your self-concept is the mental image you have of yourself. Complete the following chart with information about yourself. Then answer the questions on the next page. Your answers to these questions will help you make future career decisions.

At school:	What I Do Well	What I Enjoy Doing	What I Also Want to Do
At school:			
At work:			
At home indoors:			
At home outdoors:			
With friends:			

(Continued)

Name_____

List three adjectives your coworkers or classmates use to describe you.

_____

_____

_____

List three adjectives your teachers or supervisor use to describe you.

_____

_____

_____

How would you describe yourself?

_____

_____

_____

What are the principles, beliefs, and values you consider important?

_____

_____

Think about how your lifestyle goals will change as you complete high school and mature into adulthood. What realistic goals do you have for when you are twenty-five, forty, and sixty-five?

_____

_____

_____

_____

Abilities are skills that you possess or tasks that you can do. Check the top five strongest abilities you currently possess. Circle any skills you would like to further develop. Add any skills you possess that are not listed.

_____	Technical	_____	Public speaking
_____	Good with people	_____	Flexible
_____	Writing	_____	Responsible
_____	Mathematical	_____	Quick learner
_____	Physical	_____	Good listener
_____	Reading	_____	Creative
_____	Multilingual	_____	Communication
_____	Problem solver	_____	Motivator
_____	Organization	_____	Business sense
_____	Computer software	_____	Self-disciplined
_____	Positive attitude		

Other skills:_____

_____

Identifying Personal Interests

Activity B

Chapter 12

Name_____

Date_____Period_____

Your personal interests, abilities, and aptitudes can help you identify careers that will interest you. Look at each statement below and place a check in the column that indicates your level of interest. Then answer the questions that follow. (There are no right or wrong answers.)

	Very Much	Somewhat	No Opinion	Probably Not	No
1. I like working with people.					
2. I prefer to work alone.					
3. I like to work with animals.					
4. I like to work with plants.					
5. I prefer to work outdoors.					
6. I prefer to work indoors.					
7. I would like to explore and invent.					
8. I like science-related activities.					
9. I like creating music or playing an instrument.					
10. I want to use my design skills and ideas.					
11. I like to act.					
12. I like working with tools and machines.					
13. I like working with facts and figures.					
14. I want to sing or dance professionally.					
15. I like working with children.					
16. I like working with elderly people.					
17. I like to care for sick people.					
18. I like to paint or create artwork.					
19. I enjoy creative or report writing.					
20. I like long-range planning.					
21. I want to use my computer skills.					
22. I like selling and persuading others.					
23. I like to coach or teach others.					
24. I enjoy speaking in front of groups.					
25. I like to investigate clues and solve problems.					

(Continued)

Name_____

Choose your top five interests from the chart and list them here.

1. _____

2. _____

3. _____

4. _____

5. _____

Based on your top five interests, describe your idea of an ideal career.

_____

_____

_____

_____

_____

What aptitudes would an individual need for this career? Circle those you possess.

_____

_____

_____

_____

_____

_____

_____

_____

_____

What abilities do you need to perform well in this career?

_____

_____

_____

_____

_____

_____

_____

_____

_____

Identifying Your Personality Traits

Activity C

Chapter 12

Name_____

Date_____Period_____

Working in small groups, prepare a general list of personality traits in the space provided. Then work alone to consider your own personality traits and list them in the space below. (You may repeat personality traits from the general list.)

General Personality Traits

_____   _____   _____
_____   _____   _____
_____   _____   _____
_____   _____   _____
_____   _____   _____
_____   _____   _____
_____   _____   _____
_____

My Personality Traits

Traits I Possess   **Traits I Want to Develop**   **Traits I Need for Career Success**

_____   _____   _____
_____   _____   _____
_____   _____   _____
_____   _____   _____
_____   _____   _____
_____   _____   _____
_____   _____   _____
_____   _____   _____
_____   _____   _____
_____   _____   _____
_____   _____   _____

Matching Traits and Abilities to Jobs

Activity D   Name_____

Chapter 12   Date_____ Period_____

Work with three or four classmates to complete the following team assignment. Assume you are employees at a computer software company. Your team has been asked to analyze personality traits, abilities, and skills needed for the various positions available in your company. The information you provide will be used to develop job descriptions. Research the available jobs listed below. Then complete the information needed under each category.

Job	Personality Traits Needed	Abilities Needed	Skills/Aptitudes Needed
Computer programmer:	_____	_____	_____
	_____	_____	_____
	_____	_____	_____
	_____	_____	_____
Customer service representative:	_____	_____	_____
	_____	_____	_____
	_____	_____	_____
	_____	_____	_____
Word processor:	_____	_____	_____
	_____	_____	_____
	_____	_____	_____
	_____	_____	_____
Accountant:	_____	_____	_____
	_____	_____	_____
	_____	_____	_____
	_____	_____	_____
Sales manager:	_____	_____	_____
	_____	_____	_____
	_____	_____	_____
	_____	_____	_____

Values, Goals, Standards, and Resources

Activity E   Name_____

Chapter 12   Date_____Period_____

Relate your values, goals, standards, and resources to your future career by following the directions below.

1. List your top five values in order of priority. (There are no right or wrong answers.)

   _____ _____

   _____ _____

   _____ _____

   _____ _____

   _____ _____

2. List your career goals—three short-term goals and one long-term goal.

   Short-term goals:

   _____

   _____

   _____

   Long-term goal:

   _____

3. Describe how your career goals and values are related. _____

   _____

   _____

4. Explain whether you set high or low standards for yourself. _____

   _____

   _____

5. Explain how your standards are related to your values and goals. _____

   _____

   _____

6. List your human resources and explain how they can help in attaining your career goals. _____

   _____

   _____

   _____

7. List your nonhuman resources and explain how they can help in attaining your career goals._____

   _____

   _____

A Learning Review

Activity F   **Name**_____

Chapter 12   **Date**_____**Period**_____

Match the following terms to the correct definition. Then answer the questions below.

_____ 1. All the goods and services a person considers essential for living.

_____ 2. Something you want to achieve in a short period of time.

_____ 3. Principles and beliefs you feel are important.

_____ 4. Material things you have to achieve goals.

_____ 5. The process of taking stock of your interests, aptitudes, and abilities.

_____ 6. Something you want to achieve in the months and years to come.

_____ 7. Accepted levels of achievement.

_____ 8. Set of moral principles or values that guide a person's conduct.

_____ 9. Your skills, knowledge, and experience.

_____ 10. Doing something the same way every time.

_____ 11. What you want from your life.

_____ 12. The mental image you have of yourself.

_____ 13. A person's natural physical and mental talents for learning.

_____ 14. Physical and mental powers to perform a task or skill well.

_____ 15. How a person thinks, feels, and interacts with others.

A. self-concept
B. self-assessment
C. aptitude
D. lifestyle goals
E. ability
F. habit
G. personality
H. short-term goal
I. long-term goal
J. standards
K. standard of living
L. human resources
M. nonhuman resources
N. ethics
O. values

16. What is an example of unethical behavior? _____

_____

_____

17. What are two examples of human resources helpful in attaining career goals? _____

_____

_____

18. What methods are available for individuals to find out the aptitudes they possess? _____

_____

_____

Learning About Careers

Career Clues and Clusters

Activity A	Name_____
Chapter 13	Date_____Period_____

Read about the career clusters in Chapter 13. Then read the career clues below. Next to each career clue, identify the appropriate career cluster and career pathway.

Career Clue: Career Cluster:

1. I am a receptionist for a large corporation. _____

2. I grow apples in a large orchard. _____

3. I am a sheet-metal worker. _____

4. I am an X-ray technician at a medical center. _____

5. I care for infants in a child care center. _____

6. I design sets for the local theater. _____

7. I build houses. _____

8. I am a barber. _____

9. I manage a resort hotel. _____

10. I landscape buildings downtown. _____

11. I am a help-desk technician. _____

12. I drive a taxi. _____

13. I am a welder at a factory. _____

14. I am a paralegal. _____

15. I help people make financial plans. _____

16. I research the plant and animal life of oceans. _____

17. I am a sales representative for a food company. _____

18. I am an air traffic controller at the airport. _____

19. I am a school psychologist. _____

20. I am an economic development coordinator. _____

21. I am a firefighter. _____

22. I assist hospital patients with dietary needs. _____

23. I am a data analyst. _____

24. I enter financial data into a computer. _____

25. I am a nanny. _____

Occupation Interview

Activity B

Chapter 13

Name_____

Date_____Period_____

Choose a nontraditional occupation that appeals to you. Contact and interview a person employed in this occupation. Find out the answers to the following questions. Prepare at least two questions of your own. Discuss your interview experience in class.

Occupation:

1. How long have you worked in this occupation? _____

2. How and why did you decide on this occupation?_____

   _____

   _____

3. How and where did you obtain your training and education for this occupation? _____

   _____

   _____

4. Do you enjoy your occupation? _____

5. Would you go into this line of work again? Explain. _____

   _____

6. What advice would you give to someone considering this occupation?_____

   _____

   _____

7. Is a license or certificate required by law to work in your occupation? If so, please describe the

   procedure to obtain it. _____

   _____

8. What do you see as the future trends for this occupation?_____

   _____

   _____

9. Write two additional questions below. Then write the responses given. _____

   Question: _____

   Response:_____

   _____

   Question: _____

   Response:_____

   _____

Occupational Interests

Activity C   Name_____

Chapter 13   Date_____Period_____

For each of the 16 career clusters listed here, name and describe two occupations. Then indicate the level of education each occupation requires. Finally, place a check mark next to each occupation that interests you. (The occupations you list do not have to be those listed in the text.)

Career Cluster	Description	Education Required

Agriculture, food, and natural resources

1. _____   _____   _____

2. _____   _____   _____

Architecture and construction

1. _____   _____   _____

2. _____   _____   _____

Arts, audiovisual (A/V) technology, and communications

1. _____   _____   _____

2. _____   _____   _____

Business, management, and administration

1. _____   _____   _____

2. _____   _____   _____

Education and training

1. _____   _____   _____

2. _____   _____   _____

Finance

1. _____   _____   _____

2. _____   _____   _____

Government and public administration

1. _____   _____   _____

2. _____   _____   _____

Health science

1. _____   _____   _____

2. _____   _____   _____

Hospitality and tourism

1. _____   _____   _____

2. _____   _____   _____

(Continued)

Name_____

Human services

1. _____   _____   _____

2. _____   _____   _____

Information technology

1. _____   _____   _____

2. _____   _____   _____

Law, public safety, corrections, and security

1. _____   _____   _____

2. _____   _____   _____

Manufacturing

1. _____   _____   _____

2. _____   _____   _____

Marketing, sales, and service

1. _____   _____   _____

2. _____   _____   _____

Science, technology, engineering, and mathematics

1. _____   _____   _____

2. _____   _____   _____

Transportation, distribution, and logistics

1. _____   _____   _____

2. _____   _____   _____

Review your occupation choices. Select five that most interest you and list them below. Research your choices using the *Occupational Outlook Handbook* Web site (www.bls.gov/oco/). Describe two aspects of each occupation you find appealing.

1. _____

2. _____

3. _____

4. _____

5. _____

_____

_____

_____

_____

_____

Researching Careers

Library Research

Activity A

Chapter 14

Name_____

Date_____ Period_____

Choose two occupations and visit the library to research them. Using at least three sources of information in the library, answer the following questions.

Occupation 1: _____

Occupation 2: _____

1. What library sources of occupational information were used? _____

_____

_____

_____

2. How are the occupations described?

Occupation 1: _____

_____

_____

_____

Occupation 2: _____

_____

_____

_____

3. What is the wage or salary range?

Occupation 1: _____

_____

Occupation 2: _____

_____

4. What are the future job prospects?

Occupation 1: _____

_____

Occupation 2: _____

_____

Using the Internet

Activity B   Name_____

Chapter 14   Date_____Period_____

Using the Internet, research the occupations chosen in Activity A. Use at least three Web sites to answer the following questions.

Occupation 1: _____

Occupation 2: _____

1. What Web sites did you visit? _____

    _____

    _____

    _____

2. What other career exploration sites did you research?_____

    _____

    _____

    _____

3. What job outlook and future trends exist for each?

    Occupation 1: _____

    _____

    _____

    _____

    Occupation 2: _____

    _____

    _____

    _____

4. What training or education is needed?

    Occupation 1: _____

    _____

    _____

    _____

    Occupation 2: _____

    _____

    _____

    _____

Your Guidance Counselor

Activity C	Name_____
Chapter 14	Date_____ Period_____

Visit your guidance counselor. (If you are in the process of trying to determine a career interest, your counselor can help you to explore your options.) Research the occupations chosen in Activities A and B by discussing them with your counselor. Find answers to the following questions about the occupations you have chosen.

Occupation 1: _____

Occupation 2: _____

1. What are the entry requirements for the job?

    Occupation 1: _____

    _____

    _____

    Occupation 2: _____

    _____

    _____

2. What education or training is needed?

    Occupation 1: _____

    _____

    _____

    Occupation 2: _____

    _____

    _____

3. What schools, colleges, training programs, or registered apprenticeships offer the education you need?

    Occupation 1: _____

    _____

    _____

    _____

    Occupation 2: _____

    _____

    _____

    _____

4. Who is your guidance counselor?

    _____

Talking with Workers

Activity D	**Name**_____
Chapter 14	**Date**_____ **Period**_____

Consult workers in an informal interview to find out the following information about the occupations you have researched in Activities A, B, and C. (Conduct an informal interview with one person employed in Occupation 1 and one person employed in Occupation 2.)

Occupation 1: _____ Person contacted: _____

Occupation 2: _____ Person contacted: _____

1. Describe the duties, hours, working conditions, salary range, fringe benefits, etc.

   Occupation 1: _____

   _____

   _____

   Occupation 2: _____

   _____

   _____

2. What are the advantages and opportunities for advancement?

   Occupation 1: _____

   _____

   Occupation 2: _____

   _____

3. What are the drawbacks of the job?

   Occupation 1: _____

   _____

   Occupation 2: _____

   _____

4. What advice would you give to someone considering a job in this field?

   Occupation 1: _____

   _____

   Occupation 2: _____

   _____

   _____

   _____

Sources for Career Research

Activity E　　　　　　　　　　Name_____

Chapter 14　　　　　　　　　 Date_____Period_____

Many sources of information are available to help you research careers. A few sources of career information with certain letters missing are given below. Supply the missing letters. Then complete each statement in the space provided.

1. Informal interviews with **w** _ _ **k** _ _ _ who are in jobs that interest you can result in _____
   _____

2. Your school and local **l** _ **b** _ _ _ **r** _ _ **s** are both important sources of career information
   because_____
   _____
   _____

3. The _ **c** _ _ **p** _ **t** _ _ **n** _ **l** **O** _ _ **l** _ _ **k** _ **a** **n** _ **b** _ **o** _ is an excellent career
   information guide because _____
   _____

4. The **C** _ **r** **e** _ _ _ **u** _ **e** _ **o** **l** _ **u** **s** **t** _ _ _ **s** can be used as a companion with
   the *Occupational Outlook Handbook.* It gives individuals more information on _____
   _____

5. Using the Internet for career **r** **e** _ _ _ **a** _ **c** _ gives you access to _____
   _____

6. **D** **o** _ _ _ **t** _.gov is a Web site that has online tools for_____
   _____

7. A guidance **c** _ _ _ **n** **s** _ _ _ _ can help you explore career options by providing
   _____

8. School **c** _ **r** **e** _ _ **d** _ **y** _ let students talk to representatives of_____
   _____

Evaluating Careers

Activity F   Name_____

Chapter 14   Date_____Period_____

Evaluate the two occupations you researched in Activities A, B, C, and D by answering the questions below. When you have completed your analysis, exchange your evaluations with a classmate and review each other's work.

Occupation 1: _____

Occupation 2: _____

1. What are the general working hours?

   Occupation 1: _____

   Occupation 2: _____

2. What is the salary range?

   Occupation 1: _____

   Occupation 2: _____

3. How well does the occupation fit your personal lifestyle and goals?

   Occupation 1: _____

   _____

   _____

   Occupation 2: _____

   _____

   _____

4. How well does the occupation match your interests, aptitudes, and abilities?

   Occupation 1: _____

   _____

   _____

   Occupation 2: _____

   _____

   _____

5. Based upon your research results, how would you evaluate your ability to succeed in the occupation?

   Occupation 1: _____

   _____

   _____

   Occupation 2: _____

   _____

15 Making Career Decisions

Examining Decisions

In your own words, define the terms below. Then read the questions in the chart and determine what type of decision is needed. Write either *major* or *routine* in the middle column and explain your choice.

Definition of *major decision*:_____

_____

Definition of *routine decision*:_____

_____

Question	Type of Decision	Explanation
1. Should I get married?		
2. Which snack should I eat?		
3. What outfit will I wear today?		
4. Should I go to college?		
5. Which career is best for me?		
6. When should I go shopping?		

The Decision-Making Process

Activity B   Name _____

Chapter 15   Date _____ Period _____

Refer to the two occupations you researched in Chapter 14 for Activities A, B, C, D, and F. Using the decision-making steps below, decide which of the occupations would suit you best.

1. Define the problem (or question): _____

   _____

   _____

2. Establish your goals: _____

   _____

   _____

3. Identify your resources: _____

   _____

   _____

4. Consider the alternatives: _____

   _____

   _____

5. Make a decision: _____

   _____

   _____

6. Implement the decision (or explain how you would do this in the future): _____

   _____

   _____

7. Evaluate the results of your occupational decision. (What are some future clues that you made the right choice?): _____

   _____

   _____

   _____

   _____

   _____

   _____

   _____

   _____

Preparing a Career Plan

Activity C

Chapter 15

Name_____

Date_____Period_____

Prepare a career plan below for the career decision you made in Activity B. You may refer to the career plan shown in 15-5 in the text.

Career plan for_____

	Extracurricular and Volunteer Activities	**Work Experience**	**Education and Training**
During junior high school			
During high school			
During college			
After college			

Preparing a Career Ladder

Activity D

Chapter 15

Name_____

Date_____Period_____

Prepare a career ladder for the career decision you made in Activity B. Use the *Occupational Outlook Handbook* and the Internet for references.

Career ladder for _____

Advanced degree

Bachelor's degree

Advanced training/
associates degree

High school diploma

Part-time jobs during
high school

It's Your Decision

Activity E

Chapter 15

Name_____

Date_____ Period_____

Besides career decisions, you must also make important decisions relating to other areas of your life. The decision-making process can help you make those decisions. Think of an important decision you must make relating to your personal life, your job, or a consumer purchase. Then, apply the decision-making process described in the text.

1. Identify the problem:_____

_____

_____

2. List your goals: _____

_____

_____

3. Identify and list your resources: _____

_____

_____

4. Consider the alternatives. List the pros and cons of each choice.

Choice #1:

Pros:_____

_____

_____

_____

_____

_____

Cons: _____

_____

_____

_____

_____

_____

Choice #2:

Pros:_____

_____

_____

_____

_____

_____

Cons: _____

_____

_____

_____

_____

_____

(Continued)

Name_____

5. Make the decision: _____

_____

_____

_____

_____

6. Implement the decision. List the steps you will follow to carry out your decision:

A. _____

_____

B. _____

_____

C. _____

_____

D. _____

_____

7. Evaluate the results of your decision: _____

_____

_____

_____

_____

_____

_____

_____

8. What have you learned from applying the decision-making process to an important decision? _____

_____

_____

_____

_____

_____

_____

_____

16 Applying for Jobs

Checking Want Ads

Activity A

Chapter 16

Name _____

Date _____ Period _____

Clip two newspaper advertisements for jobs that interest you and mount them in the space below. For each, list the address, fax number, or e-mail to which résumés should be sent. If the information is given, also list the employers' names, the names of the people to contact, phone numbers, and Web sites.

Want Ad 1	Want Ad 2

Address for résumé: _____   _____

_____   _____

_____   _____

_____   _____

Fax number: _____   _____

E-mail: _____   _____

Employer name: _____   _____

Contact name: _____   _____

Phone number: _____   _____

Web site: _____   _____

Your Résumé

Activity B

Chapter 16

Name_____

Date_____ Period_____

In the space provided, design a résumé for yourself. Read it over carefully and ask your teacher or counselor to read it over as well. When you are happy with the résumé, enter it in a word processing document and print it on 8½×11-inch white bond paper. (Make copies of your résumé to submit to potential employers.)

Preparing a Portfolio

Name_____

Date_____Period_____

In the classified section of the Sunday newspaper, Jorge found an advertisement for a position as an executive assistant. Jorge phoned for an interview and plans to prepare a portfolio for it. Below is a list of items Jorge wants to put in his portfolio. Explain how each item supports Jorge's qualifications for the job described.

> Wanted: Executive assistant to a communications department manager. Exceptional organizational, writing, and computer skills.

1. Essay written in English class:_____

_____

2. Document prepared in a word processing program:_____

_____

3. Résumé:_____

_____

4. Article written for the school paper:_____

_____

5. Letter of application:_____

_____

6. Award for first place in a state spreadsheet competition:_____

_____

7. Report from a successful project completed for a club:_____

_____

8. Brochure designed on the computer:_____

_____

List the items you would include in your portfolio for one of the jobs you selected in Activity A. Explain why you selected each one.

_____

_____

_____

_____

_____

Telephoning an Employer

Activity D

Chapter 16

Name_____

Date_____ Period_____

Mindy learned that Larry's Drugstore may have a job opening. Mindy wants to apply for the job and plans to telephone the manager for an interview. Help Mindy decide how to proceed. Read the following statements about telephoning an employer. If the statement is true, write *true* in the blank. If the statement is false, write *false* in the blank.

_____ 1. Mindy's first contact with the employer may be by telephone.

_____ 2. When Mindy calls about the job lead, it does not matter if she has music playing in the background.

_____ 3. Mindy should make a list of questions she wants to ask before calling.

_____ 4. Mindy does *not* need to be ready to briefly describe her background and qualifications for the job.

_____ 5. When Mindy calls, she needs to have a pad of paper ready to take notes.

_____ 6. Mindy should use a conversational voice and good manners when she calls.

_____ 7. Mindy does *not* need to state the purpose of her call.

_____ 8. Mindy should introduce herself when she calls.

_____ 9. If during the call Mindy learns that no job opening exists, she should not waste time telling the manager she would like a job at the drugstore.

_____ 10. If Mindy does not know how to get to Larry's Drugstore, she should *not* show her ignorance by asking for directions.

Fill in the boxes below to prepare yourself for your phone conversations.

My introduction:	**My skills and qualifications:**

My background:	**Questions about the company and interview:**

Letter of Application

Activity E

Chapter 16

Name _____

Date _____ Period _____

Choose one of the job leads you listed in Activity A. In the space below, outline a letter of application for the job. Enter the letter in a word processing document and print it on 8½×11-inch white bond paper.

_____

_____

_____

_____

_____

_____

_____

_____

_____

_____

_____

_____

_____

_____

_____

_____

_____

_____

Checklist

The letter contains

_____ 1. the return address and date

_____ 2. a complete inside address

_____ 3. proper salutation

_____ 4. the first paragraph explaining that I am applying for a specific job and how I learned about it

_____ 5. the second paragraph giving information about my abilities to perform the particular job

_____ 6. the last paragraph asking for an interview and describing how I can be reached

_____ 7. a proper closing with my signature

Illegal Questions

Activity F

Chapter 16

Name _____

Date _____ Period _____

By law, an employer cannot ask certain questions on a job application form or in an interview. Read each question in the list and check *yes* if an employer can legally ask it. Check *no* if an employer cannot legally ask the question. Then provide an explanation to the last question.

Yes   No

_____   _____   1. What is your race?

_____   _____   2. Are you a U.S. citizen?

_____   _____   3. In what country were you born?

_____   _____   4. In what country were your parents born?

_____   _____   5. What is your address?

_____   _____   6. Do you attend church?

_____   _____   7. Where do you go to church?

_____   _____   8. What salary do you expect?

_____   _____   9. What are the ages of your children?

_____   _____   10. Who will care for the children while you work?

_____   _____   11. Where did you go to college?

_____   _____   12. Do you have dependable transportation?

_____   _____   13. What language do you speak at home?

_____   _____   14. When is your birthday?

_____   _____   15. What is your age?

_____   _____   16. Do you have any physical disabilities?

_____   _____   17. Where were you previously employed?

_____   _____   18. To what clubs or organizations do you belong?

_____   _____   19. Would you attach a recent photograph to your application?

_____   _____   20. Why did you leave your last job?

If an interviewer asked you an illegal question, how would you respond? Explain. _____

_____

_____

_____

_____

_____

_____

Filling Out a Job Application

Activity G

Chapter 16

Name_____

Date_____ Period_____

Application for Employment

PERSONAL INFORMATION

Date _____   Social Security Number _____

Name _____
  Last   First   Middle

Present Address _____
              Street   City   State   Zip

Permanent Address _____
              Street   City   State   Zip

Phone No. _____

If related to anyone in our employ, state name and department _____   Referred by _____

EMPLOYMENT DESIRED

Position _____   Date you can start _____   Salary desired _____

Are you employed now? _____   If so may we inquire of your present employer? _____

Ever applied to this company before? _____   Where _____   When _____

EDUCATION

	Name and Location of School	Years Completed	Subjects Studied
Grammar School			
High School			
College			
Trade, Business or Correspondence School			

Subject of special study or research work _____

(Continued)

Name_____

What foreign languages do you fluently speak? _____ Read? _____ Write? _____

U.S. Military or
Naval service _____ Rank _____   Present membership in
National Guard or Reserves _____

Activities other than religious
(civic, athletic, fraternal, etc.) _____

_____

Exclude organizations the name or character of which indicates the race, creed, color or national origin of its members _____

FORMER EMPLOYERS List employers starting with last one first

Date Month and Year	Name and Address of Employer	Salary	Position	Reason for Leaving
From				
To				
From				
To				
From				
To				
From				
To				

REFERENCES List below at least two persons not related to you whom you have known at least one year

	Name	Address	Job Title	Years Acquainted
1				
2				
3				

PHYSICAL RECORD

Have you any defects in hearing, vision or speech that might affect your job performance? _____

In case of
emergency notify _____

Name	Address	Phone No.

I authorize investigation of all statements contained in this application. I understand that misrepresentation or omission of facts called for is cause for dismissal.

Date _____   Signature _____

17 Taking Preemployment Tests

Preemployment Perception Test

Activity A

Chapter 17

Name_____

Date_____Period_____

Match the item in the first column with the answer on the right that is identical. Circle the correct match. There is only one correct response for each item. You will have exactly three minutes to complete the test.

Example			
Item	**A**	**B**	**C**
Carl E. Jones	E. Carl Jones	(Carl E. Jones)	Carl F. Jones

Item	**A**	**B**	**C**
1. Linda S. Vaughan	Linda S. Vaughan	Linda E. Vaughan	Linda S. Vaughen
2. Manuel J. Ramiz	Maneul J. Ramiz	Manuel J. Ramiz	Manuel F. Ramiz
3. $867.23	$867.23	$876.23	$867.32
4. 546-32-1145	546-23-1145	564-32-1145	546-32-1145
5. accessible	accesible	accessible	acessible
6. leisure	leisure	liesure	leisurre
7. tragedy	tragady	tragedy	tregady
8. (813) 945-3897	(813) 954-3897	(813) 945-3879	(813) 945-3897
9. commitment	comitmment	comitment	commitment
10. judgment	judgment	judgement	judgmant
11. Galaxy Systems	Galaxey Systems	Galaxy System	Galaxy Systems
12. $677.20	$667.20	$677.20	$6,777.20

Score _____

Preemployment Math Skills Testing

Name_____

Date_____Period_____

A basic math test examines a job candidate's ability to add, subtract, multiply, divide, find percentages, and work with fractions. These skills are essential for success in many work situations. Your ability to compute the answers accurately and in a set amount of time is tested here. Check the amount of time it takes you to complete the test.

Beginning time _____

Multiplication

1.   16
    × 4
	2. 69
	    × 8
		3. 36
		    × 5
			4. 79
			    × 2

Addition

5.   63
      30
      44
  + 102
	6. 44
	    57
	    60
	 + 32
		7. 24
		    43
		    29
		 + 57
			8. 37
			    63
			     3
			 + 16

9. $84.78
 + 59.50
	10. $45.08
	  + 61.01
		11. $32.12
		  + 12.18
			12. $97.65
			  + 18.24

Subtraction

13.   55
   − 32
	14. 98
	   − 73
		15. 67
		   − 19
			16. 125
			   − 31

Percentages and Fractions

17. 10% of $2,800 = _____

18. 16¾ + ¼ = _____

19. 6½ + 10½ = _____

20. 25% of $8.00 = _____

End time _____

Total time _____

Score _____

Preemployment Testing

Activity C

Chapter 17

Name_____

Date_____Period_____

Indicate what types of preemployment tests might be given for the jobs that follow. Place the appropriate letters in the blanks. (Some jobs may have more than one answer.) Then answer the questions about preemployment testing. Discuss the answers in class.

_____ 1. Administrative assistant

_____ 2. Data processing clerk

_____ 3. Auto mechanic

_____ 4. Bank teller

_____ 5. Mail carrier

_____ 6. Armed services worker

_____ 7. FBI agent

_____ 8. Airline pilot

_____ 9. Cashier

_____ 10. Professional football player

_____ 11. Clerical worker

_____ 12. Postal clerk

_____ 13. Machine operator

_____ 14. Food server

_____ 15. Office manager

A. performance skill test

B. situational skill test

C. psychological test

D. civil service test

E. Armed Services Vocational Aptitude Battery tests

F. polygraph test

G. written honesty test

H. medical examination

16. What types of preemployment tests have you taken? _____

_____

_____

_____

17. How can preemployment tests help you as well as your future employer? _____

_____

_____

_____

_____

_____

_____

_____

_____

(Continued)

Name_____

18. In what ways can you prepare yourself to take a preemployment test? _____

_____

_____

_____

_____

_____

19. How can jobs be modified for employees with the following disabilities? Explain. _____

Hearing impaired: _____

_____

_____

Visually impaired: _____

_____

_____

Physically disabled: _____

_____

_____

20. What are the advantages and disadvantages of drug testing? _____

_____

_____

_____

_____

21. How has advancements in technology changed the need for testing performance skills? _____

_____

_____

_____

_____

_____

_____

Types of Preemployment Tests

Activity D   Name_____

Chapter 17   Date_____Period_____

Read the statements below and write the missing terms in the crossword puzzle.

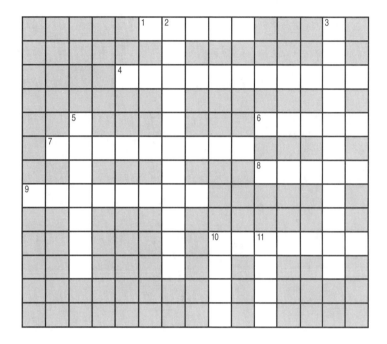

Across

1. A word processing test rates a person's _____, accuracy, and computer literacy.

4. A psychological test examines a person's _____, character, and interests.

6. The _____ is an aptitude test with a career exploration program available through the military for juniors and seniors in high school and postsecondary students.

7. Another name for a lie-detector test is a _____ test.

8. A _____ service test is an examination a person may have to take before he or she will be considered for a government job.

9. A _____ skill test is often given to applicants seeking employment as office assistants.

10. _____ examinations determine a person's physical condition for the job.

Down

2. _____ tests check your ability to operate tools and machines.

3. To test how you would actually perform on the job, you may be asked to complete a _____ test.

5. A written _____ test measures your integrity on the job.

10. A written test that checks your ability to add, subtract, and calculate is a _____ test.

11. _____ testing is used to provide a safer work environment for employees.

How to Take Preemployment Tests

Activity E   Name_____

Chapter 17   Date_____Period_____

Working in a small group, develop a checklist for preparing to take preemployment tests. Include the steps and tips an individual can use to prepare for success in taking preemployment tests. Use the information in the text as well as information from Internet searches, library resources, and your own experiences. Use the space below for your checklist.

1.

2.

3.

4.

5.

6.

7.

8.

9.

10.

18 Interviewing for Jobs

Learning About an Employer

Activity A

Chapter 18

Name_____

Date_____Period_____

Before you go on an interview, you should learn about a prospective employer. List a company for which you would like to work. Then research the company by consulting the Internet, library resources, annual reports, and other sources to find the following information.

1. Company name: _____

2. Describe the company's products or services. _____

_____

_____

_____

_____

_____

_____

_____

_____

_____

_____

_____

_____

3. How many people are employed by this company?_____

4. What are the possibilities for the growth and expansion of this company?_____

_____

_____

_____

5. How can knowing this information help you on a job interview?_____

_____

_____

_____

_____

Interview Preparation

Name_____

Date_____Period_____

Make a good impression during a job interview by preparing yourself for it. Complete the following exercise on preparing for an interview.

1. List at least four questions you would like to ask the interviewer about the job and company.

   Job: _____

   Company: _____

   Questions:

   A. _____

   _____

   B. _____

   _____

   C. _____

   _____

   D. _____

   _____

2. List items you would take with you on this interview. _____

   _____

   _____

   _____

   _____

   _____

3. Imagine you have been offered the job. List at least four questions you would ask the interviewer before accepting or rejecting the job offer.

   A. _____

   _____

   B. _____

   _____

   C. _____

   _____

   D. _____

   _____

Deciding What to Wear

Activity C

Chapter 18

Name_____

Date_____Period_____

Suppose you are going on interviews for the jobs listed below. Describe what you would wear for each interview.

1. Word processor: _____

_____

2. Bank teller: _____

_____

3. Sales associate: _____

_____

4. Auto technician: _____

_____

5. Receptionist: _____

_____

6. Stock clerk: _____

_____

7. Landscaper:_____

_____

8. Restaurant server: _____

_____

9. Construction worker:_____

_____

10. Data entry clerk:_____

_____

11. Cashier: _____

_____

12. Customer service representative:_____

_____

13. Your career goal:_____

_____

_____

Interview Questions

Activity D	**Name**_____
Chapter 18	**Date**_____**Period**_____

Before you go on an interview, it is a good idea to be prepared for the type of questions you may be asked. Questions often asked in an interview are listed below. Review each question, then answer it as you would during an interview.

1. Please tell me about yourself. _____

_____

_____

2. Why do you want to work for this company? _____

_____

3. What were your best subjects in school? _____

_____

4. What were your toughest subjects in school? What did you do to make good grades? _____

_____

_____

5. Give me an example of a complex project for which you were totally responsible. Explain what you did.

_____

_____

6. What do you see yourself doing in five years? _____

_____

_____

7. What types of jobs are you trying to avoid? _____

_____

8. What was the toughest decision you've ever made? Explain why._____

_____

_____

9. What do you do when you have trouble solving a problem? _____

_____

10. When do you like working with people and when do you prefer working alone? _____

_____

_____

11. What level of pay do you expect? _____

_____

Interviewing for a Job

Activity E

Chapter 18

Name_____

Date_____Period_____

Complete the following statements about interviewing for a job by selecting the best answer. Then explain why you have chosen that answer.

_____ 1. It is best to arrive for an interview _____.
  A. five to 10 minutes early
  B. exactly on time
  C. just a little late

Reason:_____

_____

_____ 2. Go to an interview _____.
  A. with a friend
  B. with a parent
  C. by yourself

Reason:_____

_____

_____ 3. To hide nervousness, _____.
  A. do your best to be relaxed
  B. smoke
  C. chew gum

Reason:_____

_____

_____ 4. When talking to the interviewer, _____.
  A. avoid eye contact
  B. look out the window
  C. maintain eye contact

Reason:_____

_____

_____ 5. If the interviewer asks you about your qualifications, _____.
  A. brag
  B. briefly describe your accomplishments
  C. be bashful and do not respond

Reason:_____

_____

_____ 6. If you do not know the answer to a question, _____.
  A. admit it
  B. fake it
  C. try to change the subject

Reason:_____

_____

(Continued)

Name_____

_____ 7. When speaking to an interviewer, _____.
　　　　　　　A. mumble
　　　　　　　B. speak softly
　　　　　　　C. speak clearly

Reason:_____

_____

_____ 8. If you do not have the skills for a certain job, _____.
　　　　　　　A. fake it
　　　　　　　B. admit it
　　　　　　　C. try to change the subject

Reason:_____

_____

_____ 9. If you were fired from another job, and the interviewer asks why, _____.
　　　　　　　A. lie about it
　　　　　　　B. try to change the subject
　　　　　　　C. admit the fact

Reason:_____

_____

_____ 10. The purpose of a job interview is to _____.
　　　　　　　A. brag about yourself
　　　　　　　B. convince the employer that you are the right person for the job
　　　　　　　C. beg for a job

Reason:_____

_____

_____ 11. Before accepting a job offer, you should consider _____.
　　　　　　　A. pay and fringe benefits
　　　　　　　B. how good you look in the uniform
　　　　　　　C. how long the interview was

Reason:_____

_____

_____ 12. If you decide to reject a job offer, you should _____.
　　　　　　　A. explain why you are not accepting the offer
　　　　　　　B. ignore the job offer
　　　　　　　C. wait two weeks to inform the interviewer of your decision

Reason:_____

_____

Interview Practice

Activity F

Chapter 18

Name_____

Date_____Period_____

In class, practice interviewing for a job. Have another class member role-play an employer who is interviewing you for a job. The interviewer may ask questions from Activity D or other questions appropriate for an interview. Prepare yourself as you would for an actual job interview. After completing the interview, have the interviewer evaluate you by using the following checklist. Then evaluate yourself.

Job for which you are interviewing: _____

Appearance	Yes	No
1. Clothing clean and well pressed		
2. Clothing conservative in style		
3. Body clean and odor-free		
4. Hair trimmed, clean, and combed		
5. Makeup, jewelry, and accessories used sparingly		

Behavior and Poise		
6. Reported to interview area five minutes before scheduled interview		
7. Greeted interviewer with a smile		
8. Introduced self		
9. Shook interviewer's hand		
10. Sat only when asked to do so		
11. Kept eye contact with interviewer		
12. Listened carefully to what interviewer said		
13. Considered questions carefully before answering		
14. Spoke well of previous employers and associates		
15. Showed desire to work		
16. Asked questions during interview		
17. Used proper communication skills		

Interviewer's evaluation:_____

_____

Your self-evaluation:

A. What were your strong points? _____

_____

B. What were your weak points? _____

_____

C. How could you improve your interviewing technique? _____

_____

Informational Interview Practice

Activity G   Name_____

Chapter 18   Date_____Period_____

In class, select someone who is employed in a job area that interests you and conduct an informational interview. Ask the questions below during the interview to learn more about your classmate's job and employer.

1. Where do you work? What is your job? _____

_____

2. What qualifications are needed for this job? _____

_____

_____

_____

3. Explain the career opportunities available in this job and with this employer._____

_____

_____

4. Describe your typical workweek. _____

_____

_____

_____

_____

5. According to your employer, what are your most important job responsibilities? _____

_____

_____

_____

_____

6. How many employees are in your department? _____ The company? _____

7. Describe the effectiveness of your supervisor. _____

_____

_____

8. Describe the traits of an ideal employee. _____

_____

_____

_____

The Follow-Up Letter

Activity H

Chapter 18

Name_____

Date_____Period_____

Assume you interviewed with the company you researched in Activity A. In the space below, write a follow-up letter. Then enter the letter in a word processing document and print on 8½ × 11-inch white bond paper.

_____

_____

_____

_____

_____

_____

_____

_____

_____

_____

_____

_____

_____

_____

_____

_____

_____

_____

_____

_____

Checklist

The letter contains

_____ 1. the return address and date

_____ 2. a complete inside address

_____ 3. proper salutation

_____ 4. a brief message thanking the interviewer for his or her time

_____ 5. statement about my continued interest in the job

_____ 6. a correct closing with my signature

_____ 7. (if mailed) a postmark within two days of the interview

Fringe Benefits

Activity I	Name_____
Chapter 18	Date_____Period_____

Contact an employer in your community and ask about the fringe benefits offered to employees of the company. Answer the questions below.

Company Name_____

1. Does the company provide employees with the types of insurance listed below? If so, how much coverage do the policies provide? What is the cost of the insurance to the employee?

Insurance	**Coverage**	**Cost**
Health	_____	_____
Dental	_____	_____
Life	_____	_____
Other	_____	_____

2. Does the employee receive paid vacation time? If yes, how many days per year are allowed? How long must the worker be an employee before being eligible to receive them?_____
_____

3. Does the company pay for days when an employee is sick and unable to work? If yes, how many days per year are allowed? How long must the worker be an employee before being eligible to receive them?
_____

4. Does the company provide a retirement plan? If yes, describe the plan. _____
_____
_____

5. Does the company have a profit sharing plan? If yes, describe the plan. _____
_____

6. Does the company give bonuses? If yes, when? _____
How much?_____

7. Does the company have an education reimbursement program? If yes, describe the program._____
_____
_____

8. What other benefits does the company offer? _____
_____

9. Estimate the dollar value per year of all the benefits offered by this company._____

10. Do you think this company offers a good fringe benefit package? Explain. _____
_____
_____

Succeeding on the Job

Terms for Success

Complete the following statements by filling in the blanks.

_____ 1. A new employee learns about the company's history, policies, rules, and safety procedures by attending a(n) _____.

_____ 2. A pay raise or partial payment of tuition are forms of an _____ that may be given to employees to encourage them to pursue further training.

_____ 3. Workers with a strong belief show _____.

_____ 4. _____ is a feeling of pressure, strain, or tension that results from change.

_____ 5. During a(n) _____ period, a supervisor helps train a new worker and evaluates the worker's job skills, work habits, and ability to get along with coworkers.

_____ 6. Job success depends a great deal on how your supervisor rates your _____ on the job.

_____ 7. If an employee does not perform job responsibilities as requested, the employer may _____ the employee.

_____ 8. Not showing up for work on a regular basis, which is a common reason employers give for firing employees, is called _____.

_____ 9. A job _____ is an advancement that employees must earn by being productive, cooperative, dependable, and responsible on the job.

_____ 10. A(n) _____ is a group of workers who have formed together to voice their opinions to their employer or the employer's representatives (management).

_____ 11. In workplaces with _____ _____ agreements, all workers must join the union as a condition of employment.

_____ 12. In workplaces with _____ _____ agreements, workers are free to join or not join the union.

_____ 13. _____ _____ is the process that labor and management use to discuss what they expect from each other in the workplace.

_____ 14. A(n) _____ _____ is an agreement that spells out the conditions for wages, benefits, job security, work hours, working conditions, and grievance procedures.

Starting a New Job

Activity B

Chapter 19

Name_____

Date_____ Period_____

Answer the following questions about the first day on your job.

1. Describe your first day on a new job. In your description, tell how you prepared for that day.

   _____

   _____

   _____

   _____

   _____

2. How did you learn about the company's policies and rules on your first day? _____

   _____

   _____

3. Who was responsible for your training? _____

   _____

4. What did you do to get along with your supervisor and coworkers? _____

   _____

   _____

5. According to company policy, how long is the probation period? _____

6. Imagine you are talking to a friend who is starting a new job. What advice would you give him or her about succeeding on the first day?_____

   _____

   _____

   _____

   _____

   _____

   _____

   _____

   _____

   _____

   _____

Workplace Conduct and Job Success

Activity C

Chapter 19

Name_____

Date_____Period_____

Read the following statements about workers' conduct. If the statement is an example of good conduct, write *good* in the blank. If the statement is an example of bad conduct, write *bad* in the blank.

_____ 1. They communicate well.

_____ 2. They think only of themselves.

_____ 3. They don't smile often.

_____ 4. They accept responsibility for their actions.

_____ 5. They blame others for their mistakes.

_____ 6. They respect others' opinions.

_____ 7. They don't criticize others.

_____ 8. They often complain.

_____ 9. They get along with other people.

_____ 10. They praise the company and their supervisor.

_____ 11. They enjoy working with their coworkers.

_____ 12. They are usually cheerful.

_____ 13. They have negative comments most of the time.

_____ 14. They are willing to try new tasks.

_____ 15. They believe in their ability to succeed.

_____ 16. They are grouchy and irritable.

_____ 17. They are cooperative team members.

Think of a situation in which a coworker showed poor conduct. Describe the situation. Then explain how this person's conduct could affect his or her job success._____

_____

_____

_____

_____

_____

Explain how a change of attitude can help a person show improved conduct. _____

_____

_____

_____

Handling Job Stress

Activity D   **Name** _____

Chapter 19   **Date** _____ **Period** _____

Answer the following questions about handling job stress.

1. What are three situations at work or school that you consider stressful?

   A. _____

   B. _____

   C. _____

2. What is your physical and emotional reaction to each situation?

             Physical reaction   Emotional reaction

   A. _____   _____

   B. _____   _____

   C. _____   _____

3. What are the possible causes of stress in each situation?

   A. _____

   _____

   B. _____

   _____

   C. _____

   _____

4. How did you handle each stressful situation?

   A. _____

   _____

   B. _____

   _____

   C. _____

   _____

5. What are four other ways to handle job stress effectively?

   A. _____

   B. _____

   C. _____

   D. _____

Job Satisfaction

Activity E
Chapter 19

Name_____

Date_____ Period_____

Indicate whether you agree or disagree with each statement in the chart and provide an explanation. Then complete the sentence below.

Statement	Agree or Disagree	Reasons
1. I seem to be making progress in my job.		
2. I get personal satisfaction from my job.		
3. I feel I am paid adequately for the work I do.		
4. My work is challenging.		
5. There are opportunities for advancement in this job.		
6. This job offers me security.		
7. I perform a variety of work activities.		
8. This job gives me a feeling of accomplishment.		
9. This job allows me to make good use of my skills.		
10. This job allows me to make good use of my education and training.		
11. I am willing to accept responsibility.		
12. I am in the best job for me.		

To me, job satisfaction means _____

_____

_____

How Am I Doing?

Activity F   Name_____

Chapter 19   Date_____ Period_____

Review each question in the chart and rate your own job performance. Be honest and fair with yourself as you analyze the good and bad aspects of your work performance. Then write what you can do to change or improve. (There are no right or wrong answers.)

Work Performance	Yes	Sometimes	No	Recommendations for Improvement
1. Do I get to work late?				
2. Do I have a good attendance record?				
3. Can I do my job well?				
4. Is my work high quality?				
5. Do I work well without supervision?				
6. Am I honest by not loafing or stealing company time or supplies?				
7. Am I loyal to my employer?				
8. Am I cooperative with my supervisor and my coworkers?				
9. Do I make a favorable personal impression?				
10. Do I keep myself well groomed?				
11. Do I practice safe working habits?				
12. Do I take proper care of my employer's equipment and materials?				

(Circle one.)

Overall, I rate my job performance as: Excellent   Very good   Acceptable   Fair   Poor

Changing Jobs

Activity G   Name_____

Chapter 19   Date_____Period_____

Interview someone who has changed jobs and ask that person the following questions. Then ask two questions of your own. Discuss the interview in class.

1. Why did you change jobs? _____

   _____

   _____

2. Did you take a job with a different employer? If you stayed with the same employer, was it a lateral move or promotion?_____

   _____

   _____

3. Do you feel you make the right decision by changing jobs? _____

   _____

   _____

   _____

   _____

   _____

4. What advice would you give someone who is considering a job change? _____

   _____

   _____

   _____

   _____

   _____

5. Question: _____

   _____

   Response:_____

   _____

   _____

6. Question: _____

   _____

   Response:_____

   _____

   _____

Unions

Activity H

Chapter 19

Name_____

Date_____**Period**_____

Interview someone who is a union member and ask that person the following questions. Then ask one question of your own. Discuss the interview in class.

1. Is union membership a requirement for your job? If not, why did you choose to become a union member?

   _____

   _____

2. Is union membership required of all employees at your job? _____

3. Of which union are you a member? _____

4. Who is your immediate union representative/leader? _____

5. How does a person become a union representative/leader?_____

   _____

   _____

6. How much are the union dues? _____

7. What are the benefits of union membership? _____

   _____

   _____

   _____

8. Do you feel that the benefits of union membership are worth the cost? Explain. _____

   _____

   _____

   _____

9. What does the union contract cover? _____

   _____

   _____

   _____

   _____

10. Question: _____

   _____

   Answer: _____

   _____

   _____

20 Diversity and Rights in the Workplace

My Heritage

Activity A

Chapter 20

Name_____

Date_____ Period_____

Interview a grandparent or another older relative. Ask the relative to recall being your age as he or she answers the following questions. Record the answers in the space provided and be prepared to discuss your interview in class.

Name of interviewee: _____

Relationship of interviewee to me: _____

Age

Most children attended school until age _____

Children were considered grown and ready to become independent when they reached the age of _____

_____

The age at which most couples married was _____

Gender Issues

The household tasks handled by females consisted of_____

_____

_____

The household tasks handled by males consisted of _____

_____

_____

The jobs open to adult females included _____

_____

_____

The jobs open to adult males included _____

_____

_____

Only men were allowed to _____

_____

Women were expected to _____

_____

(Continued)

Name_____

Language

The primary language spoken at home was_____

The primary language spoken at school was_____

_____

_____

The language(s) spoken in banks, stores, and other public places was (were)_____

_____

Family, Culture, and Traditions

My birthplace is (city, state/region, and country)_____

_____

I grew up in (city, state/region, and country)_____

_____

My parents made a living by_____

_____

Besides my sisters, brothers, and parents, the family members living with us included_____

_____

The holidays and special events we always celebrated included_____

1. _____
2. _____
3. _____
4. _____
5. _____
6. _____
7. _____
8. _____

The foods always served at family gatherings included_____

_____

_____

_____

Religion

The houses of worship in my community included (List types, not specific names.)_____

_____

_____

Diversity Awareness

BLaBLaBLa

Activity B

Chapter 20

Name _____

Date _____ Period _____

True/False: Circle *T* if the statement is true or *F* if the statement is false.

T F 1. Diversity involves respecting people's differences.

406 ✗ T F 2. When diversity is supported, everyone is allowed to maintain his or her individuality.

T F 3. Mexico is the most diverse country in the world because its population comes from every other nation.

406 ✗ T F 4. The diversity of the U.S. population is most evident in small rural towns.

406 ✗ T F 5. There is a natural tendency to seek out and stay close to people who are like yourself.

T F 6. Throughout history, conflicts have arisen when groups of people who are alike have tried to change those who are different.

T F 7. Factors that cause population differences include cultural heritage, race, gender, and religion.

T F 8. Cultural heritage determines what beliefs, learned behaviors, and language pass through the generations to each individual.

T F 9. Not all Americans are part of an ethnic group.

T F 10. When different cultures associate, there is the opportunity to share the best of what each has to offer.

T F 11. Today, assimilation is considered the best way to handle diverse populations.

402 T F 12. When employers, employees, and customers speak different languages, misunderstandings often result.

T F 13. Problems in the workplace may arise over off-time granted for observing the practices of one religion but not others.

T F 14. The number of older workers in society is quickly decreasing.

T F 15. Everyone is a potential candidate for some form of disability during his or her life.

409 ✗ T F 16. Companies have found that teaching employees to value workers' differences yields negative results.

409 ✗ T F 17. Employees feel more comfortable in the workplace when the emphasis is on who they are, not what they contribute.

409 ✗ T F 18. When all ideas are valued, people feel greater freedom to make suggestions and present alternative views.

T F 19. If sensitive issues can be raised without fear of hurting coworkers' feelings, decisions can be made faster.

410 ✗ T F 20. A diverse workforce understands a wider range of customers.

414 ✗ T F 21. Over half of all working-age women are employed outside the home.

415 ✗ T F 22. Companies can avoid conflict by having one religious display reflecting the beliefs of most people in the company.

416 ✗ T F 23. Unskilled older workers may have difficulty keeping their jobs.

416 ✗ T F 24. Disabled workers can be productive and dependable.

T F 25. Having a policy of accepting diversity can help a company gain public respect.

Promoting Diversity

Activity C

Chapter 20

Name_____

Date_____Period_____

Working in small groups, accomplish the team assignment for promoting diversity described below.

Team assignment: Your group is in charge of designing a program to promote diversity in the community or in one team member's workplace. Before developing a plan, check what others in similar situations are doing. You may gather this information from interviews, the Internet, and library sources. List below the top three ideas that your team considered most worthwhile and develop your program using one of them. Explain below the details of your program and how it would work.

What were the team's top three ideas for a diversity program? (List first the number 1 idea on which the team's program is based.)

1. _____

_____

2. _____

_____

3. _____

_____

Where would the team's diversity program be used? (Who is the target audience?) _____

_____

_____

What types of printed material(s) would be used? (Describe it/them.) _____

_____

_____

How would the target audience receive the program message?_____

_____

_____

What signs should your team see if the plan is successful? _____

_____

What might be some signs that the plan is *not* successful? _____

_____

_____

Know Your Rights

Activity D   Name_____

Chapter 20   Date_____Period_____

Listed below are a variety of employment situations. Read each situation and answer the questions using information on workplace rights provided in the chapter.

1. Jerome was born in Uruguay to United States citizens. Jerome's family moved to Florida when he was twelve years old. After completing high school, Jerome applied for a position as welding apprentice at a local company. He was not considered for the apprentice position because of his birth location. The employer was unsure of Jerome's citizenship status.

   What federal law or guidelines cover this situation? _____

   _____

   What is the first thing Jerome should do? _____

   _____

   _____

2. Amanda is an entry-level software engineer at a large company. After overhearing a conversation involving her boss, Amanda discovered that her starting salary was $2,000 less than a man who held a similar position. Both positions had the same requirements regarding skill and responsibility.

   What federal law or guidelines cover this situation? _____

   _____

   What is the first thing Amanda should do?_____

   _____

   _____

3. Tracey, who works at a busy office processing mortgage applications, is paid minimum wage. Often customers call just before closing time, which forces Tracey to work after her assigned 40 hours. Tracey has been frustrated when she receives her weekly paycheck because she is paid only for 40 hours.

   What federal law or guidelines cover this situation? _____

   _____

   What is the first thing Tracy should do?_____

   _____

   _____

4. Maya wears a small dot on her forehead. The dot is a symbol worn by female members of her religion. Her employer has asked her to cover the dot when she is working at the front counter assisting customers.

   What federal law or guidelines cover this situation? _____

   _____

   What is the first thing Maya should do?_____

   _____

   _____

(Continued)

Name_____

5. Heidi applied by phone for a position at a nearby clothing store for a part-time position during the Christmas season. The ad in the paper stated that no experience was necessary. Heidi spoke to the person responsible for hiring over the phone and felt she had an excellent chance at employment. When Heidi arrived at the store in her wheelchair to complete the application, the spokesperson said all positions were filled. The next week, Heidi saw another ad in the local newspaper for employment opportunities at that same store. She felt she might not have been hired because of her disability.

What federal law or guidelines cover this situation? _____

_____

What is the first thing Heidi should do? _____

_____

_____

6. Allie works in the service department of an automobile dealership. In the break room, posters and calendars are posted showing women in swimsuits. Allie feels uncomfortable going into the break room because of these pictures. Usually when she passes through the break room, her coworkers comment on her figure and suggest a job as a calendar swimsuit model. Allie does not want any further discussion about it.

What federal law or guidelines cover this situation? _____

_____

What is the first thing Allie should do? _____

_____

_____

7. Francesca's native language is Spanish. She was excited to find a coworker from the Caribbean at her place of employment. At breaks and lunch, Francesca and her new friend speak in Spanish to each other. Francesca's supervisor has requested Francesca to only speak English at work because other coworkers feel uncomfortable hearing a different language.

What federal law or guidelines cover this situation? _____

_____

What is the first thing Francesca should do? _____

_____

_____

8. At age 55, Leona is looking for a new job. She was laid off from her job at a telephone company where she received numerous awards for outstanding work during her twenty years in the accounting department. Leona is becoming very discouraged in her job search after receiving ten rejection letters this week. She thinks that her age is the reason for a lack of job offers. She also thinks her layoff from the telephone company was due to her age.

What federal law or guidelines cover this situation? _____

_____

What is the first thing Leona should do? _____

_____

_____

Diversity Terms

Activity E

Chapter 20

Name _____

Date _____ Period _____

Complete the following word puzzle by filling in the correct terms. Then answer the question at the bottom of the page and discuss your answer in class.

```
1              _  _  _  D  _  _
2           _  _  _  _  I  _  _  _
3              _  _  V  _  _
4              _  _  E
5           _  _  _  _  R  _  _  _  _  _  _  _  _  _
6           _  _  S  _  _  _  _  _  _  _  _  _
7           _  _  _  I  _  _
8              _  T  _  _  _  _
9  _  _  _  _  _  _  _  Y  _  _
```

1. Women face sex discrimination, or _____ bias, when they are restricted from training opportunities and higher-paying jobs.

2. _____ penalties, including a jail sentence or fine, may result from interfering with a person's employment rights.

3. The 1964 _____ Rights Act banned employment discrimination on the basis of race, color, religion, sex, or national origin.

4. The across-the-board firing of people over 40 to allow younger, less costly employees to fill the jobs is an example of _____ discrimination.

5. Treating people on a basis other than individual merit.

6. Blending people into society by helping, and sometimes forcing, them to become more like the majority.

7. The belief that one race is superior or inferior to all others.

8. A group of people who share common racial and/or cultural characteristics is a(n) _____ group.

9. A label given to a person based on assumptions held about all members of that person's racial or cultural group.

10. What strategies are used at your school or workplace to promote diversity?

_____

_____

_____

_____

_____

Harassment Points

Activity F

Chapter 20

Name_____

Date_____Period_____

Fill in the chart below using the information about sexual harassment in your text.

5 things I know about harassment:	**4** things that discourage harassment:	**3** actions to take when harassment happens:
1.	1.	1.
2.	2.	2.
3.	3.	3.
4.	4.	
5.		

21 Succeeding in Our Economic System

Another Economic System

Activity A

Chapter 21

Name_____

Date_____Period_____

Interview someone who has lived under an economic system that is different from the free enterprise system of the United States. (A foreign exchange student could be a good resource person.) Find out the following information. Discuss the interview in class.

1. Person interviewed: _____

2. Country:_____

3. Type of economic system: _____

4. Describe life under the economic system of this person's country: _____

_____

_____

_____

_____

_____

_____

_____

_____

_____

_____

5. Describe the major differences between this economic system and the free enterprise system of the United States: _____

_____

_____

_____

_____

_____

_____

_____

_____

_____

Business in a Free Enterprise System

Activity B

Chapter 21

Name_____

Date_____Period_____

Interview a business owner to find answers to the following questions. Discuss your findings in class.

1. Name of business: _____

2. Is this business a proprietorship, partnership, or corporation? _____

3. How long has the business existed? _____

4. What does this business produce or what service does it provide? _____

   _____

   _____

5. How does supply and demand affect this business? _____

   _____

   _____

   _____

   _____

6. What competitors does this business have?_____

   _____

   _____

7. How does this business compete?_____

   _____

   _____

8. In what way is the government involved with this business (through controls, regulations, etc.)? _____

   _____

   _____

9. What is the structure of this business? Describe it. _____

   _____

   _____

10. How many employees (part-time and full-time) work here? _____

   _____

11. What outside consultants, such as accountants and attorneys, are used?_____

   _____

   _____

The Competitive Business World

Activity C

Chapter 21

Name_____

Date_____Period_____

Competition encourages businesses to make quality goods and services available at lower prices. Working with a small group, research the price of a handheld global positioning navigation system (GPS) from four different sources. Include a local business, mail-order catalog, and Web site in your search. Then answer the questions below. Compare your findings with other teams in your class.

Features desired in GPS system: _____

Source	Price	Additional Charges	Delivery Time
1. _____	_____	_____	_____
2. _____	_____	_____	_____
3. _____	_____	_____	_____
4. _____	_____	_____	_____

Where is the best place to purchase the GPS? _____

Why? _____

_____

_____

_____

What factors affect the costs of the GPS? _____

_____

_____

_____

How do supply and demand affect the cost of the GPS? _____

_____

_____

_____

_____

_____

In the next five years, from which source do you think most people will purchase a GPS system? Explain.

_____

_____

_____

Free Enterprise System

Activity D

Chapter 21

Name_____

Date_____Period_____

Match each definition below with the correct term from the word bank.

Word Bank

capital	free market	productive
competition	government	profit
corporation	monopoly	proprietorship
demand	needs	supply

_____ 1. The desire for _____ motivates businesses to produce the goods and services consumers want.

_____ 2. A _____ is a single company that controls the entire supply of a product or service.

_____ 3. _____, labor, land, and equipment are productive resources used to produce and provide goods and services.

_____ 4. _____ encourages businesses to produce quality goods and services at low prices.

_____ 5. The amount of products and services available for sale is called the _____.

_____ 6. The basics a person must have to live are called _____.

_____ 7. The total amount of products and services consumers want to buy is called _____.

_____ 8. In a _____, people have the right to decide how and where to earn, spend, save, and invest their money.

_____ 9. Some _____ involvement is required to keep our economic system free and fair.

_____ 10. _____ resources are all resources used to produce goods and services.

_____ 11. A business that has only one owner is a _____.

_____ 12. A _____ is a business owned by many people that have purchased stock in the company.

Forms of Business Ownership

Activity E

Chapter 21

Name_____

Date_____Period_____

In the following statements, match the form of business ownership with the appropriate description. Then fill the chart below with examples from your community. Name two businesses for each form of ownership listed. Be prepared to explain your decisions to the class.

_____ 1. Steven is a stockholder in an international oil company.

_____ 2. When Mary Elman died, the business she and Veronica Glass owned jointly was dissolved.

_____ 3. Lee Clausen operates a fast-food business specializing in submarine sandwiches. Lee receives all the profits that are made.

_____ 4. Randy Grier's interest in baseball player cards evolved into a small business out of his home.

_____ 5. Although she does not work with her friend, Barbara invested money in her friend's beauty salon.

_____ 6. Dave's company plans to expand the business and produce more goods by selling stocks to investors.

_____ 7. Al's interest and experience in woodworking and art led him to start his own retail framing business.

_____ 8. Marta and her brother plan to operate their father's dry cleaning business after his retirement.

A. sole proprietorship

B. partnership

C. corporation

Businesses in the Community	
Type of Ownership	**Name**
Proprietorship	1.
	2.
Partnership	1.
	2.
Corporation	1.
	2.

Business Structures

Activity F
Chapter 21

Name _____

Date _____ Period _____

Prepare an organization chart showing the management structure that exists where you work (or at your school). Begin with the top managerial position and show the organizational levels down through lower-level employees. Explain the structure in class.

Employer's name: _____

Type of management structure: _____

(Diagram of business structure:)

22 Entrepreneurship: A Business of Your Own

Importance of Small Business

Activity A

Chapter 22

Name_____

Date_____Period_____

Read the following statements about small businesses. If the statement is true, circle *T*. If it is false, circle *F* and rewrite the statement on the line below to make it true.

T F   1. Businesses owned by entrepreneurs help keep the economy strong by creating jobs.

_____

_____

T F   2. Small businesses compete only against small corporations.

_____

_____

T F   3. The overall standard of living increases when more people work.

_____

_____

T F   4. Small businesses employ a third of all U.S. workers not employed by government.

_____

_____

T F   5. Some small businesses provide specialized products that large corporations do not.

_____

_____

T F   6. The economy of the United States does *not* rely on small business owners.

_____

_____

T F   7. Small businesses account for few of the innovative products and services.

_____

_____

T F   8. Small businesses help keep prices in line.

_____

_____

Exploring Entrepreneurship

Activity B   Name _____

Chapter 22   Date _____ Period _____

Interview an entrepreneur in your community. Find out the answers to the questions below. Write two additional questions of your own. Discuss the interview in class.

Name of entrepreneur: _____

Name of business: _____

1. What product or service do you sell? Explain why you decided to work in this type of business. _____
   _____
   _____

2. How long have you been in business? _____

3. How did you start the business? _____
   _____
   _____

4. What personal skill or knowledge is most needed to start this type of business? _____
   _____

5. What form of business ownership do you have now? _____

6. Why did you choose to locate your business in its present location? _____
   _____
   _____

7. How many hours do you work weekly? _____

8. What do you see as the greatest advantage of having your own business? _____
   _____

9. What do you dislike most about being your own boss? _____
   _____

10. Question: _____
    Response: _____
    _____
    _____

11. Question: _____
    Response: _____
    _____
    _____

Qualities for Success

Activity C

Chapter 22

Name_____

Date_____Period_____

Do you have what it takes to succeed as an entrepreneur? Listed below are some of the qualities successful entrepreneurs possess. Place a check mark next to the qualities you believe you possess. Then answer the questions that follow.

Qualities I Possess:

_____

_____

_____

_____

_____

_____

_____

_____

_____

_____

_____

_____

_____

_____

_____

_____

_____

Motivating Goals

- to pursue a dream
- to make noteworthy achievements
- to be profitable
- to have total control
- to use all skills and talents
- to surpass the efforts of peers

Personality

- self-starter
- self-assured
- outgoing
- efficient
- risk-taker
- optimistic

Aptitudes/Abilities

- sets goals and makes plans
- innovative
- organized
- solves problems well
- people-oriented
- understands basic financial matters

1. What do you feel are the most important qualities for an entrepreneur to have? _____

_____

_____

_____

_____

(Continued)

Name_____

2. Would you like to be an entrepreneur? Explain._____

_____

_____

_____

_____

3. Who are entrepreneurs in your community? List their names and describe their businesses._____

_____

_____

_____

_____

_____

_____

_____

_____

_____

_____

_____

_____

_____

_____

4. Considering your interests, abilities, and work experiences, what type of business might you like to run?

_____

_____

_____

_____

_____

_____

_____

5. How would you evaluate your likelihood of becoming an entrepreneur? Place a check next to the one statement that best describes your evaluation.

_____ I definitely want to have my own business in the future.

_____ I am very interested in starting a business, but I need more experience first.

_____ I am not interested in starting my own business, but I could change my mind.

_____ I want to work for an established employer.

Planning a Business

Activity D

Chapter 22

Name_____

Date_____Period_____

Suppose you want to become an entrepreneur. To help you start planning this business, complete the following information. Then report your business plan to the class.

1. Describe the business you would start. _____

_____

_____

_____

_____

2. Identify the product or service your business would offer._____

_____

_____

_____

_____

3. List your skills and experience that relate to the business. _____

_____

_____

_____

4. Indicate the potential success for the business. (Consider potential customers, the competition, and your sales ability.)_____

_____

_____

_____

5. Indicate a location for the business._____

_____

6. What factors would you consider in establishing a price for your product or service? _____

_____

_____

_____

7. What form of business structure would you choose? Why?_____

_____

_____

_____

(Continued)

Name_____

8. Identify any zoning laws that would regulate your business operation. _____

_____

_____

_____

9. Identify governmental licenses or permits needed. _____

_____

_____

10. Explain how you would obtain financing to get a business started. _____

_____

_____

11. Indicate the capital expenses needed to start the business. (Consider equipment and supplies you will need.)

_____

_____

_____

_____

_____

12. What type of record-keeping system would you use? Why? _____

_____

_____

13. What professional assistance would you seek to help start and operate the business? _____

_____

_____

_____

14. What weaknesses in your plan could cause the business to fail?_____

_____

_____

_____

15. What strengths in your plan could make the business a success?_____

_____

_____

_____

_____

(Continued)

Name_____

16. Using your responses from questions 2 through 11, develop a start-up business plan.

My Business Plan

_____
_____
_____
_____
_____
_____
_____
_____
_____
_____
_____
_____
_____
_____
_____
_____
_____
_____
_____
_____
_____
_____
_____
_____
_____
_____
_____
_____
_____
_____
_____
_____
_____

Entrepreneurship Terms

Activity E

Chapter 22

Name_____

Date_____Period_____

Complete each sentence by using a term from the word bank.

Word Bank

assets	fixed	innovative	overhead
break-even point	flexible	liabilities	profit ratio
capital	franchise	loan	receipts
commission	fraud	location	zoning laws

_____ 1. Your _____ include all the money you receive from your customers for cash and credit sales.

_____ 2. _____ expenses are one-time costs needed to get the business started.

_____ 3. Items that a business owns are called _____.

_____ 4. The ability to come up with new ideas is being _____.

_____ 5. The _____ of a business could determine the success of the business.

_____ 6. _____ _____ regulate what types of business activities can be performed in certain areas.

_____ 7. When planning a business, you would need to contact a financial institution to arrange for a(n) _____.

_____ 8. A(n) _____ is the right to market another company's product or service.

_____ 9. A(n) _____ is a percentage of sales paid to a salesperson.

_____ 10. Examples of _____ expenses would be monthly rent payments and garbage pickup.

_____ 11. People who rush into businesses are prime victims of franchise and business _____.

_____ 12. Rent, utilities, office supplies, postage, and advertising are all examples of _____ expenses.

_____ 13. _____ expenses are those that vary from month to month.

_____ 14. The _____-_____ _____ is when the income of a business equals expenses.

_____ 15. Any debts that you owe are called _____.

_____ 16. Your _____ _____ is the percentage of your receipts that are profit.

Understanding Income and Taxes

Forms of Income

Activity A

Chapter 23

Name_____

Date_____Period_____

Read the statements below and write the missing terms in the crossword puzzle.

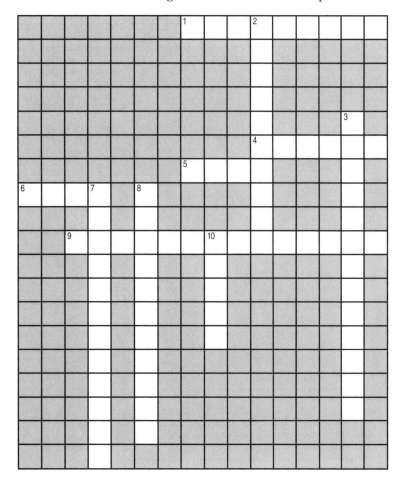

Across

1. A fixed amount of money for each piece of work done.
4. A set amount of money paid for a certain period of time.
5. Small amounts of money given by customers to service-related workers in return for good service.
6. A set amount of pay for every hour worked.
9. Extra financial rewards, such as holidays, sick leave, and profit sharing. (two words)

Down

2. A percentage of money taken in from sales made.
3. Profits returned to employees who create greater profit for the company through their hard work. (two words)
7. Money you receive for doing a job. (two words)
8. The lowest amount of money an employer is allowed by law to pay per hour. (two words)
10. An extra payment in addition to a worker's regular pay.

Understanding Your Paycheck

Activity B

Chapter 23

Name_____

Date_____Period_____

Stephen works full-time during the summer at a local fast-food restaurant. He just received his first paycheck. Use the paycheck stub below to answer the following questions about his paycheck.

1. Identify the important parts of his paycheck in the space provided.

A. _____   B. _____   C. _____

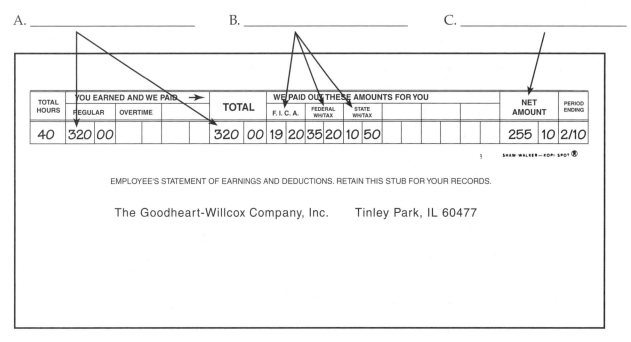

TOTAL HOURS	YOU EARNED AND WE PAID ➞				TOTAL		WE PAID OUT THESE AMOUNTS FOR YOU						NET AMOUNT		PERIOD ENDING
	REGULAR	OVERTIME					F. I. C. A.	FEDERAL WH/TAX	STATE WH/TAX						
40	320 00				320	00	19 20	35 20	10 50				255	10	2/10

EMPLOYEE'S STATEMENT OF EARNINGS AND DEDUCTIONS. RETAIN THIS STUB FOR YOUR RECORDS.

The Goodheart-Willcox Company, Inc.   Tinley Park, IL 60477

2. What was Stephen's gross pay? _____

3. How much were the total deductions made from his paycheck?_____

4. What was Stephen's net pay? _____

5. How many hours did Stephen work last week? _____

6. What is his hourly wage? _____

7. When Stephen started his job, his employer asked him to fill out Form W-4. Why?_____

_____

_____

8. Stephen is single and is claimed on his parents' tax return as an exemption. Can Stephen claim himself as an exemption on his Form W-4? Explain. _____

_____

9. What social security taxes were deducted? _____

10. What other types of deductions could be taken out of Stephen's paycheck? _____

_____

_____

Types of Taxes

Activity C   Name_____

Chapter 23   Date_____ Period_____

Five types of taxes are listed below. Match each type of tax to its description. (The types of taxes may be used more than once. There may be more than one answer for each description.)

_____ 1. A tax on a person's income.

_____ 2. A tax placed on certain products such as gasoline or cigarettes.

_____ 3. Examples of direct taxes.

_____ 4. A tax on goods and services.

_____ 5. An example of a progressive tax.

_____ 6. Taxes withheld from a paycheck by an employer, as determined by the information provided on the Employee's Withholding Allowance Certificate by the employee.

_____ 7. A tax placed on certain products or services such as telephone service or liquor.

_____ 8. In some states, food and drugs may be exempt from this tax.

_____ 9. This tax is an example of an indirect tax.

_____ 10. This tax is an example of a regressive tax.

A. personal income tax
B. social security tax
C. property tax
D. sales tax
E. excise tax

Tax Opinions

Activity D
Chapter 23

Name_____

Date_____ Period_____

For each statement below, indicate whether you agree or disagree by circling one of the terms. Explain your decisions and be prepared to discuss your opinions with the class. (There are no right or wrong answers.)

1. Income tax is the fairest tax. (Agree, Disagree) Explain. _____

_____

_____

_____

_____

2. A sales tax is not fair to some groups in a community. (Agree, Disagree) Explain. _____

_____

_____

_____

_____

3. An excise tax on gasoline is a fair tax. (Agree, Disagree) Explain._____

_____

_____

_____

_____

4. Everyone should pay the same taxes regardless of their income level. (Agree, Disagree) Explain. _____

_____

_____

_____

_____

5. The government makes good use of our tax dollars. (Agree, Disagree) Explain. _____

_____

_____

_____

_____

6. Paying taxes is necessary so the government can operate smoothly. (Agree, Disagree) Explain._____

_____

_____

_____

Preparing Tax Returns

Activity E

Chapter 23

Name_____

Date_____Period_____

Answer the following questions.

1. Joel works at his uncle's sporting goods store, volunteering a few hours a week to help keep financial records straight. Is he required to file a federal income tax return? Explain._____

   _____

   _____

2. Too much tax was withheld from Cheryl's paychecks during the year. What will happen when she files her federal income tax return?_____

   _____

3. Not enough tax was withheld from Larry's paycheck during the year. What will happen when Larry files his federal income tax return? _____

   _____

4. Which of the following must you list as income on your tax return? Check the correct answer(s). _____

   _____ wages   _____ tips   _____ salaries   _____ bonuses

5. Lisa is preparing her federal income tax return. What is a legal way she can avoid paying some or all of her taxes?_____

   _____

   _____

6. Roy failed to declare all his income and falsified his deductions, adjustments, and credits on his income tax return. What has Roy committed? _____

   _____

7. Steve wants to get extra copies of federal income tax return forms. Where can he obtain them?_____

   _____

   _____

8. What financial records might Marsha need in order to file an accurate federal income tax return? _____

   _____

   _____

   _____

   _____

   _____

   _____

   _____

Government Insurance Programs

Activity F

Chapter 23

Name _____

Date _____ Period _____

Complete the following statements by filling in the blanks.

_____ 1. The federal government's program for providing income when a family's earnings are reduced or stopped because of retirement, disability, or death is called _____ _____.

_____ 2. The purpose of social security is to provide a(n) _____ level of income that people can build on with savings, pensions, investments, or other insurance.

_____ 3. You must have earned a certain number of social security _____ before you can receive social security benefits.

_____ 4. Workers may retire as early as age _____, but they will receive lower retirement benefits.

_____ 5. Workers born after 1959 become eligible for full retirement benefits at age _____.

_____ 6. A worker who becomes severely disabled before age 65 can receive _____ checks.

_____ 7. If a worker dies, _____ benefits can be paid to certain members of the worker's family.

_____ 8. When a person becomes eligible for social security benefits, he or she must _____ for them at the nearest social security office.

_____ 9. The social security tax is figured as a(n) _____ of an employee's income.

_____ 10. _____ _____ _____ pays benefits to individuals with disabilities who have few possessions or little money.

_____ 11. The _____ program was created to provide older citizens and people with disabilities with affordable health insurance.

_____ 12. The _____ program was created to provide health care services to low-income people who are unable to pay for them.

_____ 13. The _____ _____ program was created to provide payments to workers if they are injured on the job.

_____ 14. Under workers' compensation, _____ programs provide funding for retraining workers who must give up their jobs because of injury.

_____ 15. _____ _____ provides benefits to workers who have lost their jobs through no fault of their own.

 **Managing Spending**

Managing Your Money

Activity A

Chapter 24

Name_____

Date_____ Period_____

Complete the following open-ended statements about budgeting your money and being an informed consumer.

1. Now that I'm earning an income, I plan to_____

_____

_____

2. In the future, I want to be able to buy _____

_____

_____

3. To make the most of the dollars I earn, I _____

_____

_____

4. Of the many possible forms of payment (cash, checks, credit cards, etc.), I tend to use_____

_____

5. If I see something I want to buy but do not have enough cash, I would probably_____

_____

6. When I buy a product or service that does not live up to the claims advertised, I _____

_____

7. To me, a budget is_____

_____

8. The definition of a smart shopper is _____

_____

_____

9. The shopping advice I carefully listen to is _____

_____

10. An example of the type of shopping advice I ignore is _____

_____

Fixed and Flexible Expenses

Activity B

Chapter 24

Name_____

Date_____ Period_____

Complete the following exercise about fixed and flexible expenses.

1. Define *fixed expenses*. _____

_____

_____

2. Define *flexible expenses*._____

_____

_____

3. The following items could appear on your budget. Indicate those items that are fixed expenses and those that are flexible expenses by placing a check in the appropriate column.

Products and Services	Fixed Expenses	Flexible Expenses
Bus fare	_____	_____
Books	_____	_____
Car repair	_____	_____
Doctor bill	_____	_____
Groceries	_____	_____
Insurance premium	_____	_____
Medicine	_____	_____
Movie	_____	_____
Raincoat	_____	_____
Rent	_____	_____
Savings	_____	_____
Car payment	_____	_____
Phone bill	_____	_____
Bowling	_____	_____
Summer school	_____	_____

Preparing a Budget

Activity C

Chapter 24

Name_____

Date_____Period_____

Prepare a monthly budget for yourself. Then evaluate the budget. You may use the form below or prepare your own on a separate sheet of paper.

Monthly Budget		
Goals	Approximate Cost	Date to achieve goal
Short-range _____	$_____	_____
_____	_____	_____
Long-range _____	_____	_____
_____	_____	_____

Income		**Fixed Expenses**	
		Description	Amount
Salary	$_____	_____	$_____
Interest on savings	_____	_____	_____
Interest on investments	_____	_____	_____
Part-time work	_____	_____	_____
Other	_____	**Flexible Expenses**	
		_____	_____
		_____	_____
		_____	_____
		_____	_____
Total Income:	$_____	**Total Expenses:**	$_____

1. Do you have enough income to cover your expenses?_____

2. Is the budget flexible enough to handle unexpected expenses? _____

3. Is your money doing what you want it to do? _____

4. Is your budget helping you reach important goals on schedule?_____

5. If you answered *no* to any of the questions above, what changes should you make in your budget? ____

_____

_____

_____

_____

Advertising

Activity D

Chapter 24

Name_____

Date_____Period_____

Use the Internet, newspapers, and magazines to find advertisements for the products and services listed below. For each advertisement, place a check in the appropriate column to indicate the promotional method used. Then answer the questions that follow.

	Special Sales	Promotions	Buying Incentives
Food	_____	_____	_____
Clothing	_____	_____	_____
Furniture	_____	_____	_____
Photo printing	_____	_____	_____
Automobile	_____	_____	_____
Hair or nail care	_____	_____	_____
Phone service	_____	_____	_____
Electronic equipment	_____	_____	_____

1. What is the purpose of advertising?

_____

_____

2. Do any of your advertisements appear misleading? If so, explain how. _____

_____

_____

_____

_____

3. Did any of the ads try to persuade you to buy products or services you do not need, do not want, or cannot afford? If so, which? _____

_____

_____

4. How can consumers use ads to make wise buying decisions?_____

_____

_____

_____

_____

Where to Shop?

Activity E

Chapter 24

Name _____

Date _____ Period _____

Several products are listed in the chart below. Decide where you would prefer to shop for each product. Place a check in the appropriate column to indicate your choice. Then answer the questions that follow.

Products:	Department Store	Discount Store	Specialty Store	Factory Outlet	Catalog Mail-Order/TV	Direct Mail	Internet
Fashionable clothing	_____	_____	_____	_____	_____	_____	_____
Greeting cards	_____	_____	_____	_____	_____	_____	_____
Brand-name running shoes	_____	_____	_____	_____	_____	_____	_____
Perfume or cologne	_____	_____	_____	_____	_____	_____	_____
Microwave oven	_____	_____	_____	_____	_____	_____	_____
Prom dress or tuxedo rental	_____	_____	_____	_____	_____	_____	_____
Desk	_____	_____	_____	_____	_____	_____	_____
School supplies	_____	_____	_____	_____	_____	_____	_____

1. Choose three products from the chart above. Explain what factors affected your shopping decisions for each.

   A. _____

   _____

   _____

   B. _____

   _____

   _____

   C. _____

   _____

   _____

2. Of the many types of shopping sites available, which type do you prefer? Explain. _____

   _____

   _____

   _____

Comparison Shopping

Activity F

Chapter 24

Name_____

Date_____Period_____

Comparison shopping helps you save money, get better quality, and find the products that best suit your needs. Select one item you would like to purchase. Comparison shop in three different stores. Complete the chart below with your shopping information. Then answer the questions that follow.

Item:_____

	Location 1	Location 2	Location 3
Name of store	_____	_____	_____
Location/site	_____	_____	_____
Price of item	_____	_____	_____
Key features (model number, brand, etc.)	_____	_____	_____
	_____	_____	_____
	_____	_____	_____
	_____	_____	_____
	_____	_____	_____
Quality	_____	_____	_____
Selection	_____	_____	_____
Customer services available	_____	_____	_____
Warranty	_____	_____	_____

1. Using the information from your chart, where would you purchase the item?_____

   _____

   Explain your choice._____

   _____

   _____

   _____

   _____

2. How does comparison shopping help you avoid impulse buying? _____

   _____

   _____

   _____

   _____

The Right Way to Complain

Activity G

Chapter 24

Name _____

Date _____ Period _____

For each statement below, circle *T* if it is true or *F* if it is false.

T   F   1. When a product or service is not satisfactory, you have the right to recourse.

T   F   2. If you drop your new camera and break it, you have the right to complain.

T   F   3. If you discover a problem with a purchase, it is best to wait several weeks before contacting the seller or manufacturer.

T   F   4. If your problem cannot be settled by a store manager, you should write a letter to the company's consumer affairs department.

T   F   5. A threatening letter is more likely to get results.

T   F   6. At the close of a complaint letter, you should state what you would like done about the problem.

T   F   7. If you fail to get satisfactory results from your complaint, you may need to contact an appropriate consumer organization or government agency for help.

T   F   8. A consumer organization can force a business to accept the solution it recommends.

T   F   9. The Better Business Bureau (BBB) is a nonprofit organization sponsored by private businesses.

T   F   10. The BBB tries to settle consumer complaints against local businesses.

T   F   11. The BBB *cannot* release information on other consumer complaints against a business.

T   F   12. A consumer action group consists of a panel of people who try to judge your complaint fairly.

T   F   13. Government agencies have the authority to take action against dishonest businesses.

T   F   14. Federal agencies oversee the licensing of service facilities such as hospitals or nursing homes.

T   F   15. The CPSC can require a product recall on products found to be dangerous.

T   F   16. The CPSC regulates the production, packaging, and labeling of cosmetics.

T   F   17. The FDA helps prevent unfair competition, deceptive trade practices, and false advertising.

T   F   18. Problems with mail orders, warranties, and deceptive advertising can be referred to the FTC.

T   F   19. Problems with phone, TV, and cable operators can be referred to the FCC.

T   F   20. Filing a lawsuit should be the last resort for settling a complaint.

Complaint Letter

Activity H

Chapter 24

Name_____

Date_____Period_____

Assume you are the consumer in the case described below. Using the facts given, compose a complaint letter to send to the store's general manager, Ms. Nakisha Jones. Write only the salutation and body of that letter in the box.

Case Study: On June 16, 20xx, you purchased a cell phone for $199.00. When the salesperson demonstrated the phone in the store, the reception was excellent, but at home it was poor. You returned the cell phone for a refund on the following day to the store manager on duty, Mr. Sydney Washington. You explained the reason for the return, but Mr. Washington checked the phone and said it was fine. He refused to refund your money or exchange the cell phone. You are unhappy with the cell phone and your problem has not been settled.

Complaint Form

Activity I

Chapter 24

Name _____

Date _____ Period _____

When a product you have purchased is not satisfactory, you have the right to recourse. Imagine you are the consumer in the case below. Complete the following form using the information given.

Case Study: On February 10, 20xx, you purchased an MP3 player at Super Items, 111 South Adams Street, Anytown, IL 33614. It was advertised in your local newspaper on February 8. The advertised features included "easy to operate," 8GB built-in memory, battery life up to 22 hours for music playback, and "satisfaction guaranteed." You bought it for the advertised price of $199.99. Later at home, you found the navigation screen difficult to operate. That same day, you returned the MP3 player for a refund to Mr. Mike Hensley, the store manager on duty. You pointed out the problem, but Mr. Hensley disagreed that a problem existed. As a result, he refused to refund your money or exchange the MP3 player. You are unhappy with the MP3 player and your problem has not been settled. You have decided to file a complaint with the local Better Business Bureau.

Better Business Bureau of Chicago and Northern Illinois

Chicago, Illinois 60611

COMPLAINT FORM

PLEASE FOLLOW ENCLOSED INSTRUCTIONS

Date of Transaction _____ Date You Complained to Company _____ To Whom _____

Sales Person _____ Identify Product/Service _____ If Advertised, When _____

Where (Enclose Ad) _____ Receipt, Contract, or Policy Number _____

COMPANY _____   YOUR NAME _____

ADDRESS _____   ADDRESS _____

CITY _____   CITY _____
        State   Zip Code   State   Zip Code

YOUR EMPLOYER'S FIRM NAME: _____ YOUR DAYTIME PHONE NO. _____

BRIEFLY EXPLAIN YOUR COMPLAINT AND FOLLOW THE ENCLOSED INSTRUCTIONS:

_____

_____

_____

_____

_____

_____

_____

_____

_____

_____

What Adjustment Do You Consider Mutually Fair?

_____

                                               Your Signature   Date

Avoiding Consumer Fraud

Activity J   Name_____

Chapter 24   Date_____Period_____

Read the cases below and determine whether they are legitimate consumer contacts or examples of phishing or vishing. Explain your answers.

1. Jennifer has a Suncoast credit card. Their official Web site is www.suncoast.com. Jennifer received an e-mail from Suncoast credit cards with the following message:

   Save up to hundreds of dollars by transferring your high-interest balances to your Suncoast credit card. Use our _savings calculator_ to determine how much money you can save. Act quickly because this offer expires April 30, 20xx. _Click here_ to learn more. _Click here to transfer balances now_. (The hyperlinks open www.suncoast.com.)

   _____

   _____

2. Patrick has an internet account with Quicknet. Their official Web site is www.quicknet.com. He received the following e-mail from Quicknet-Database using the address information-quicknet@billing.org.

   As a valued Quicknet customer, this e-mail is being sent to inform you that your Quicknet account information has expired. Unless you update your account information immediately, we will be forced to block access to your account. To update your account _click here_ (www.quicknet-reactivation.net).

   _____

   _____

3. Lorena received a telephone call from a person claiming to be a customer service representative from First Bank. The representative tells Lorena there is a problem with her account and gives her a toll free number to call to straighten out the problem.

   _____

   _____

4. Jestina received a telephone call from a person claiming to be a customer service representative from Holland National Bank. The representative explains that they have received a request for payment from Martin's Jewelry Store for $516.45 for a bracelet purchased on March 3, 20xx. The representative is calling to verify that Jestina made this purchase. He does not ask for her account number or other personal or financial information.

   _____

   _____

25 Using Credit

Understanding Credit

Activity A

Chapter 25

Name _____

Date _____ Period _____

Complete the following exercise to check your knowledge of credit.

1. Define *credit*. _____

_____

2. Explain how to determine your debt-to-income ratio. _____

_____

3. What does it mean to establish credit? _____

_____

_____

4. Why is it important to establish good credit? _____

_____

_____

5. What is a credit rating? _____

_____

6. What does it mean when a person is called a good credit risk? _____

_____

7. What traits do creditors consider when deciding if you are a good credit risk? _____

_____

_____

8. List the advantages of using credit. _____

_____

_____

_____

9. List the disadvantages of using credit. _____

_____

_____

_____

(Continued)

Name_____

10. Name the six types of credit available to consumers._____

_____

_____

11. Explain how a revolving charge account works._____

_____

_____

12. What is the difference between a charge account and an installment account? _____

_____

_____

_____

13. Why must a borrower pledge something of value as collateral to get a cash loan?_____

_____

_____

14. What are the first steps you could take to establish credit?_____

_____

_____

15. What information is included in a credit record? _____

_____

_____

16. What is the purpose of a credit bureau?_____

_____

_____

17. Why is it important to carefully examine a credit agreement before you sign it? _____

_____

18. What should you do if you have a problem getting credit?_____

_____

_____

19. If you ever have a problem paying your bills on time, what should you do about your creditors? _____

_____

_____

20. What should you do if your credit card is lost or stolen?_____

_____

_____

Applying for Credit

Activity B

Chapter 25

Name _____

Date _____ Period _____

Complete the following credit application form. Then answer the questions that follow.

SEARS, ROEBUCK AND CO. INDIVIDUAL CREDIT ACCOUNT APPLICANT

APPLICATION TO BE COMPLETED IN NAME OF PERSON IN WHICH THE ACCOUNT IS TO BE CARRIED.

COURTESY TITLES ARE OPTIONAL   PLEASE PRINT

☐ MR.   ☐ MRS.   ☐ MISS   ☐ MS. _____
                                          First Name   Initial   Last Name

Street Address   City   State   Zip Code

Phone No: Phone No: Soc. Sec.   Number of
Home _____   Business _____   No. _____   Age ____   Dependents _____
                                                                                                (Excluding Applicant)

Are you a United States citizen?   ☐ Yes   ☐ No   If NO, explain immigration status: _____

_____

How Long at   Monthly Rent or
Present Address _____   Own ☐   Rent-Furnished ☐   Rent-Unfurnished ☐   Board ☐   Mortgage Payments $ _____

Name of   Street   City
Landlord _____   Address _____   and State _____

Former Address (if less than 2   How
years at present address) _____   long _____

Employer _____   Street   City
                                     Address _____   and State _____

How   Net   Monthly ☐
long _____ Occupation _____   Income $ _____   Weekly ☐

Former Employer   How
(If less than 1 year with present employer) _____   long _____

ALIMONY, CHILD SUPPORT, OR SEPARATE MAINTENANCE INCOME NEED NOT BE REVEALED IF YOU DO NOT WISH TO HAVE IT CONSIDERED AS A BASIS FOR PAYING THIS OBLIGATION.

Alimony, child support, separate maintenance received under:

☐ Court order   ☐ Written agreement   ☐ Oral understanding   Amount $ _____

Other income, if any: Amount $ _____   Source _____

                                                                        Savings ☐   Acc't No. _____
Name and Address of Bank _____   Checking ☐   Acc't No. _____
                                                                        Loan ☐   Acc't No. _____

Previous   ☐ Yes   Is Account ☐ Yes   Date Final
Sears Account   ☐ No _____   _____   Paid in Full ☐ No   Payment Made _____
                      At What Sears Store   Account No.

Relative or
Personal Reference
Other than Spouse _____
                      (Name)   (Street Address)   (City and State)   (Relationship)

(Continued)

Name_____

<table>
<tr><td colspan="2">**CREDIT REFERENCES**
Attach additional sheet if necessary</td><td colspan="4">List all references
(Open or closed within past two years)</td></tr>
<tr><td>Charge Accounts
Loan References
Store/Company Address</td><td>Date
Opened</td><td>Name Account
Carried in</td><td>Account
Number</td><td>Balance</td><td>Monthly
Payments</td></tr>
<tr><td></td><td></td><td></td><td></td><td></td><td></td></tr>
<tr><td></td><td></td><td></td><td></td><td></td><td></td></tr>
<tr><td></td><td></td><td></td><td></td><td></td><td></td></tr>
<tr><td></td><td></td><td></td><td></td><td></td><td></td></tr>
</table>

Authorized buyer _____
                First Name   Initial   Last Name   Relationship to applicant

Authorized buyer _____
                First Name   Initial   Last Name   Relationship to applicant

SEARS IS AUTHORIZED TO INVESTIGATE MY CREDIT RECORD AND TO VERIFY MY CREDIT, EMPLOYMENT AND INCOME REFERENCES.

SIGNATURE OF APPLICANT X _____ DATE _____

THE INFORMATION BELOW IS REQUIRED IF: (1) YOUR SPOUSE IS AN AUTHORIZED BUYER OR (2) YOU RESIDE IN A COMMUNITY PROPERTY STATE (ARIZONA, CALIFORNIA, IDAHO, LOUISIANA, NEVADA, NEW MEXICO, TEXAS, WASHINGTON) OR (3) YOU ARE RELYING ON THE INCOME OR ASSETS OF ANOTHER PERSON, INCLUDING A SPOUSE OR FORMER SPOUSE, AS A BASIS FOR PAYMENT.

Name of spouse ☐
Name of former spouse ☐ _____
Name of other person ☐
                          Address   Age

                     Street   City
Employer _____ Address _____ and State _____

How   Soc. Sec.   Net   Monthly ☐
long _____ Occupation _____ No. _____ Income $ _____ Weekly ☐

                                       Savings ☐   Acc't No. _____
Name and Address of Bank _____ Checking ☐   Acc't No. _____
                                       Loan ☐   Acc't No. _____

THE PERSON ON WHOSE INCOME OR ASSETS YOU ARE RELYING AS A BASIS FOR PAYMENT MUST SIGN BELOW. HOWEVER, YOUR SPOUSE NEED NOT SIGN IF YOU RESIDE IN A COMMUNITY PROPERTY STATE OR IF YOUR SPOUSE IS AN AUTHORIZED BUYER.

SEARS IS AUTHORIZED TO INVESTIGATE MY CREDIT RECORD AND TO VERIFY MY CREDIT, EMPLOYMENT AND INCOME REFERENCES.

X _____
(Signature of person on whose income or   Date
assets applicant is relying.)

Based on the information you have given in this application, would you consider yourself to be a good credit risk? Explain. _____

_____

_____

_____

_____

_____

What steps could you take to build a good credit rating? Explain. _____

_____

_____

_____

_____

Cost of Credit

Activity C

Chapter 25

Name_____

Date_____Period_____

Read the following story about Nancy. Then answer the questions that follow.

> **Case Study:** Nancy decided to purchase a new television on credit. The selling price of the television is $650.00. The salesperson told Nancy the store would finance the television for one year at an annual percentage rate of 15 percent or for two years at a rate of 12 percent. Nancy must decide which option to take.

1. Define *finance charge*. _____

   _____

2. How much interest will Nancy pay if she finances the television for one year? _____

3. How much interest will Nancy pay if she finances the television for two years? _____

4. What is the total cost of the television if she finances it for one year?_____

5. What is the total cost of the television if she finances it for two years?_____

6. By law, what are creditors required to tell Nancy concerning her finance charges?_____

   _____

7. Would you advise Nancy to finance the television for one year or for two years? Explain. _____

   _____

   _____

   _____

   _____

   _____

   _____

   _____

   _____

   _____

8. Do you think the television is worth the price Nancy must pay? Why? _____

   _____

   _____

   _____

9. How else might Nancy purchase the television? _____

   _____

   _____

   _____

Federal Credit Laws

Activity D

Chapter 25

Name_____

Date_____Period_____

Six federal credit laws are listed below. Match each law to its description(s). (The laws may be used more than once.)

    A. Truth in Lending Act
    B. Fair Credit Reporting Act
    C. Equal Credit Opportunity Act
    D. Fair Credit Billing Act
    E. Electronic Funds Transfer Act
    F. Fair Debt Collection Practices Act

_____ 1. Prohibits a creditor from denying credit on the basis of sex, marital status, race, religion, age, or for receiving public assistance.

_____ 2. Requires creditors to send customers a written explanation of steps to take when a billing error or question occurs.

_____ 3. Requires creditors to tell customers the cost of credit before they use it.

_____ 4. Can limit your liability if you report a lost or stolen credit card promptly.

_____ 5. Provides for confidentiality of information contained in credit reports.

_____ 6. Protects consumers against unfair billing.

_____ 7. Limits a cardholder's liability to $50 if a lost or stolen credit card is used by someone else.

_____ 8. Provides for accuracy of information contained in credit reports.

_____ 9. Prohibits businesses from issuing or mailing credit cards to people who have not requested them.

_____ 10. Protects consumers from abusive, unfair, or deceptive conduct by collection agencies.

_____ 11. Applies to the use of computers, ATMs, debit cards, and other electronic banking transactions.

_____ 12. Prohibits collection agencies from revealing or publicizing a debtor's debt to other people.

_____ 13. Limits loss to $50 if you notify the institution within two days of a lost or stolen credit card.

Using Credit Wisely

Activity E

Chapter 25

Name_____

Date_____Period_____

Identify an item you would like to buy on credit. Contact three creditors and compare the credit terms available from them to allow you to purchase the item. Then answer the following questions about using credit wisely.

Item _____

Creditor 1. Name of Business: _____

1. What is the size of the loan?   _____

2. What is the APR for the loan?   _____

3. What is the repayment time?   _____

4. What is the total cost of the loan plus the interest?   _____

Creditor 2. Name of Business: _____

1. What is the size of the loan?   _____

2. What is the APR for the loan?   _____

3. What is the repayment time?   _____

4. What is the total cost of the loan plus the interest?   _____

Creditor 3. Name of Business: _____

1. What is the size of the loan?   _____

2. What is the APR for the loan?   _____

3. What is the repayment time?   _____

4. What is the total cost of the loan plus the interest?   _____

1. Based on your comparison, would you purchase the item on credit? Why or why not? _____

_____

_____

2. From which creditor would you purchase the item? _____

Why? _____

_____

_____

_____

(Continued)

Name_____

3. If you do not purchase the item on credit, how could you pay for it? _____

_____

_____

4. What are some signs of credit problems?_____

_____

_____

_____

5. If you lose control of your credit and cannot afford to make your payments, what should you do? _____

_____

_____

6. How can credit counseling help you with credit problems?_____

_____

_____

_____

7. What is bankruptcy? _____

_____

_____

_____

8. What is the difference between Chapter 7 bankruptcy and Chapter 13 bankruptcy? _____

_____

_____

_____

_____

9. If you purchase an item under a finance plan that offers "no finance charges for six months," what happens when you have not paid off the loan in full in the seventh month?_____

_____

_____

_____

10. What steps could you take to assure that you do not have finance charges when you purchase an item under the terms "no finance charges for six months"? _____

_____

_____

_____

26 Banking, Saving, and Investing

Compare Financial Institutions

Activity A

Chapter 26

Name_____

Date_____Period_____

Working in groups, survey three local financial institutions about the services they offer by finding out the information below. Decide on one type of banking account to compare at these financial institutions. Complete the questions that follow. Make a presentation to the class about your research.

Type of account: _____

	Minimum Balance	Age Requirement	Charges	Interest Rates
Institution 1 (name):				
Institution 2 (name):				
Institution 3 (name):				

1. What other types of accounts are offered by the above financial institutions? _____

_____

_____

_____

(Continued)

Name_____

2. Are any special services available to customers at these financial institutions?

   Institution 1: _____

   _____

   Institution 2: _____

   _____

   Institution 3: _____

   _____

3. What are the policies and charges for using automatic teller machines (ATMs)?

   Institution 1: _____

   _____

   Institution 2: _____

   _____

   Institution 3: _____

   _____

4. Why is it important to know the insurance policies the financial institutions have? _____

   _____

   _____

5. Which institution did your team prefer? Explain. _____

   _____

   _____

   _____

   _____

   _____

   _____

   _____

   _____

6. How can choosing the right financial institution help you manage money effectively? _____

   _____

   _____

7. What conveniences has online banking provided for consumers? _____

   _____

   _____

Checks

Activity B

Chapter 26

Name_____

Date_____ Period_____

Every number and word on a check is important. Identify the information on the checks below in the spaces provided.

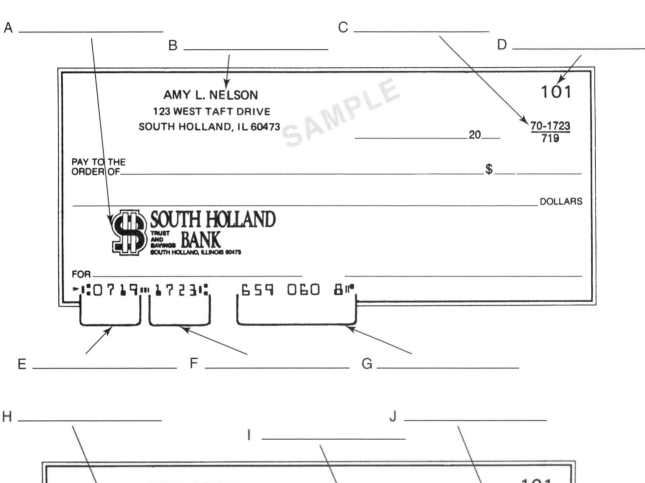

A _____

B _____

C _____

D _____

AMY L. NELSON
123 WEST TAFT DRIVE
SOUTH HOLLAND, IL 60473

SAMPLE

_____ 20___

101

70-1723
719

PAY TO THE
ORDER OF_____ $_____

_____ DOLLARS

SOUTH HOLLAND
TRUST AND SAVINGS BANK
SOUTH HOLLAND, ILLINOIS 60473

FOR _____

⑆0719⑈1723⑆ 659 060 8⑉

E _____

F _____

G _____

H _____

I _____

J _____

AMY L. NELSON
123 WEST TAFT DRIVE
SOUTH HOLLAND, IL 60473

September 7 20XX

101

20
70-1723
719

PAY TO THE
ORDER OF *Sleep-Rite Furniture* _____ $ *255.17*

Two Hundred Fifty-Five and 17/100 _____ DOLLARS

SOUTH HOLLAND
TRUST AND SAVINGS BANK
SOUTH HOLLAND, ILLINOIS 60473

FOR *Mattress*

⑆0719⑈1723⑆ 659 060 8⑉

Amy L. Nelson

K _____

L _____

M _____

Using a Checking Account

Activity C   Name_____

Chapter 26   Date_____ Period_____

Terry Johnson has a checking account at South Holland Trust and Savings Bank. Assume you are Terry Johnson and complete the following banking transactions.

Making a Deposit

You want to deposit $43.00 in currency, $2.78 in coins, a check in the amount of $28.55, and a check in the amount of $98.29. Using this information and today's date, fill out this deposit slip.

DEPOSIT TICKET

TERRY JOHNSON
123 W. TAFT DRIVE
SOUTH HOLLAND, IL 60473

DATE_____20_____

CASH	CURRENCY	
	COIN	
LIST CHECKS SINGLY		
TOTAL FROM OTHER SIDE		
TOTAL		
LESS CASH RECEIVED		
NET DEPOSIT		

70-1723/719

USE OTHER SIDE FOR ADDITIONAL LISTING

BE SURE EACH ITEM IS PROPERLY ENDORSED

$$ SOUTH HOLLAND TRUST AND SAVINGS **BANK** SOUTH HOLLAND, ILL. 60473

⑆071917232⑆ ⑈616⑊765⑈6⑈

DE LUXE NO 1   CHECKS AND OTHER ITEMS ARE RECEIVED FOR DEPOSIT SUBJECT TO THE PROVISIONS OF THE UNIFORM COMMERCIAL CODE OR ANY APPLICABLE COLLECTION AGREEMENT

Writing a Check

Write a check for $35.24 to pay for books purchased at Webster's Bookstore. Use today's date.

TERRY JOHNSON   **237**
123 W. TAFT DRIVE
SOUTH HOLLAND, IL 60473   _____20_____ 70-1723/719

PAY TO THE
ORDER OF_____| $ _____

_____DOLLARS

$$ SOUTH HOLLAND TRUST AND SAVINGS **BANK** SOUTH HOLLAND, ILL. 60473

MEMO_____   _____

⑆071917232⑆ ⑈616⑊765⑈6⑈

(Continued)

Name_____

Filling Out a Check Register

Record the amounts of your deposit and the check to Webster's Bookstore in this register. Your previous balance was $185.64.

RECORD ALL CHARGES OR CREDITS THAT AFFECT YOUR ACCOUNT							BALANCE	
NUMBER	DATE	DESCRIPTION OF TRANSACTION	PAYMENT/DEBIT (–)	✓ T	FEE (IF ANY) (–)	DEPOSIT/CREDIT (+)	$	
			$		$	$		

Balancing a Bank Statement

Your bank statement shows a closing balance of $299.67. Both the deposit you made earlier and the check you wrote in this activity are not shown on the statement. Also, you have five additional outstanding checks: $13.37 (#228), $51.30 (#230), $7.32 (#231), $25.00 (#232), and $17.04 (#235). Use this information to fill in this worksheet. The balance on the worksheet should be the same as the balance above in the check register.

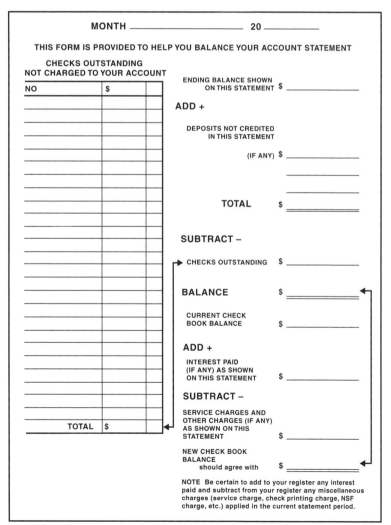

MONTH _____ 20 _____

THIS FORM IS PROVIDED TO HELP YOU BALANCE YOUR ACCOUNT STATEMENT

CHECKS OUTSTANDING
NOT CHARGED TO YOUR ACCOUNT

NO	$	

ENDING BALANCE SHOWN
ON THIS STATEMENT $ _____

ADD +

DEPOSITS NOT CREDITED
IN THIS STATEMENT

(IF ANY) $ _____

_____

TOTAL $ _____

SUBTRACT –

CHECKS OUTSTANDING $ _____

BALANCE $ _____

CURRENT CHECK
BOOK BALANCE $ _____

ADD +

INTEREST PAID
(IF ANY) AS SHOWN
ON THIS STATEMENT $ _____

SUBTRACT –

SERVICE CHARGES AND
OTHER CHARGES (IF ANY)
AS SHOWN ON THIS
STATEMENT $ _____

TOTAL $ _____

NEW CHECK BOOK
BALANCE
should agree with $ _____

NOTE Be certain to add to your register any interest paid and subtract from your register any miscellaneous charges (service charge, check printing charge, NSF charge, etc.) applied in the current statement period.

Safe-Deposit Boxes

Activity D

Chapter 26

Name_____

Date_____Period_____

In the list of items below, check those that should be stored in a safe-deposit box. Then answer the questions that follow.

_____ 1. Birth certificate

_____ 2. Checkbook

_____ 3. Driver's license

_____ 4. Will

_____ 5. Title of car ownership

_____ 6. Check stubs

_____ 7. Precious jewelry

_____ 8. Deeds to property

_____ 9. Credit cards

_____ 10. Stocks

_____ 11. Bank statements

_____ 12. Bonds

_____ 13. Insurance policies

_____ 14. Old gold coins

_____ 15. Social security card

16. What is the purpose of using a safe-deposit box?_____

_____

_____

_____

17. What are the policies (rates, hours of accessibility, security measures, etc.) for using a safe-deposit box at a financial institution in your community? Name the institution and describe the policies. _____

_____

_____

_____

_____

_____

_____

_____

Investing Your Money

Activity E

Chapter 26

Name_____

Date_____Period_____

Read the statements below and write the missing terms in the crossword puzzle.

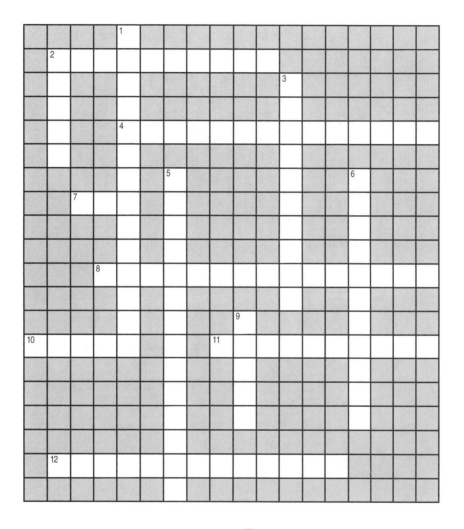

Across

2. Stocks, bonds, and mutual funds.
4. Bonds issued by a corporation. (two words)
7. A tax-deferred retirement savings plan.
8. Bonds that are more a source of savings than an investment. (two words)
10. Certificates of debt or obligation issued by a corporation or government.
11. An investment in land or building property. (two words)
12. Investments in a variety of securities such as preferred stock, common stock, and bonds. (two words)

Down

1. Bonds issued by state, county, or city government. (two words)
2. A share of ownership in a corporation.
3. A company that collects money from a number of investors and invests that money in securities. (two words)
5. A type of stock that is a more conservative investment and involves less risk. (two words)
6. A type of stock that involves more risk. (two words)
9. A tax-deferred retirement plan for self-employed people or employees of unincorporated companies that do not have their own pension plan.

Banking and Investment Terms

Activity F

Chapter 26

Name_____

Date_____Period_____

Complete the following statements by filling in the blanks.

_____ 1. _____ banks are often called full-service banks because of their many services.

_____ 2. In most commercial banks and savings banks, the money you deposit is safe because it is insured by the _____ for up to $100,000.

_____ 3. A savings _____ offers many of the same services provided by commercial banks.

_____ 4. A(n) _____ _____ differs from a commercial bank and a savings bank in that its services are for its members only.

_____ 5. Most credit unions are insured by the _____.

_____ 6. A(n) _____ _____ _____ authorizes your bank to electronically pay certain bills directly from your account each month.

_____ 7. A(n) _____ _____ _____ can be used to withdraw money from your account when you are shopping in the mall.

_____ 8. In order to use an ATM, you must have a(n) _____.

_____ 9. You may pay for purchases in a store without cash, check, or credit cards by using a(n) _____ _____.

_____ 10. _____ checking works very well for people who use online banking, banking by phone, or ATMs to do all their banking.

_____ 11. A(n) _____ _____ is good to have if you want an interest-bearing account and can maintain the minimum balance.

_____ 12. A(n) _____-_____ checking account allows you to earn interest and write checks on the same account.

_____ 13. When two or more people share a bank account, it is called a(n) _____ account.

_____ 14. A check with a(n) _____ endorsement can be cashed by anyone who possesses it.

_____ 15. *For deposit only* is a common _____ check endorsement.

_____ 16. A(n) _____ _____ is a record of the checks, deposits, and charges made to your account for a specific length of time.

_____ 17. If you are going to be traveling, _____ checks are convenient to use.

_____ 18. If you are paying a large sum of money, a(n) _____ check may be a more acceptable form of payment than a personal check.

_____ 19. A(n) _____ check is a personal check with a bank's guarantee that the check will be paid.

_____ 20. If you do not have a checking account, you can use a(n) _____ _____ to make a payment safely by mail.

_____ 21. _____-_____ _____ are small metal containers people rent to protect their valuables from fire and theft.

_____ 22. A(n) _____ savings account is a convenient form of savings, but it pays the lowest rate of interest.

_____ 23. With a(n) _____ _____ _____, you deposit money for a set period of time and earn a set annual rate of interest.

27 Insurance

Auto Insurance

Activity A

Chapter 27

Name _____

Date _____ Period _____

Read the following cases about auto insurance. Then answer the questions related to each case. Discuss the cases and answers in class.

Case 1: Kevin talked to his insurance agent about buying auto insurance. The agent gave several examples of the types of problems Kevin might have and how auto insurance could protect him. Indicate which type of auto insurance would cover each possible problem.

A. bodily injury liability

B. property damage liability

C. medical payments

D. uninsured/underinsured motorists

E. comprehensive

F. collision

_____ 1. During a rainstorm, Kevin swerves to miss a dog, runs into a fence, and damages it.

_____ 2. A compact disc, books, and tools are stolen from Kevin's car.

_____ 3. As Kevin drives his friend Juan to school, another driver runs a stop sign and hits Kevin's car. Both Kevin and Juan are injured. The driver of the other car does not have insurance.

_____ 4. Kevin runs into a telephone pole, causing $700 worth of damage to the front of his car.

_____ 5. Coming home from a party, Kevin daydreams and runs into another car. The people in that car are injured.

_____ 6. Kevin is injured in a car accident.

Case 2: When Latrice bought her car from a used car dealer, he suggested a local insurance company to her. She took his advice and bought insurance with the company. She thought the premiums seemed high for the amount of coverage she would receive, but she did not want to take the time to talk to other companies. Latrice's father was angry when she told him about the insurance she had purchased. "Why did you not shop around? Why did you not compare premiums and coverages?" he asked.

1. What factors determine Latrice's insurance premium rate? _____

_____

_____

2. What are some questions Latrice should ask the next time she shops for insurance? _____

_____

3. Why is it important to shop around and compare premiums and coverages? _____

_____

(Continued)

Name_____

Case 3: John plans to buy an old used pick-up truck. Although the truck runs fairly well, the body is in bad shape. John says, "I will only carry collision insurance. I do not need bodily injury or property damage liability coverage."

1. Was John right in his decision? Explain. _____

_____

_____

_____

2. What advice would you give to John?_____

_____

_____

_____

Case 4: Julie plans to spend most of her money on a nice car. She says she will not have enough money left to buy insurance. "I will drive extra careful until I can afford to buy auto insurance," she says.

1. Can Julie drive a car without buying auto insurance? Explain. _____

_____

_____

2. What problems could Julie have because she does not have auto insurance? _____

_____

_____

_____

3. What is the best thing for Julie to do until she can afford auto insurance? _____

_____

_____

_____

_____

Case 5: Maurice is involved in an automobile accident with his friend William. Both are players on the school's basketball team, on their way to a championship game. They decide to get to the game on time and handle details about the accident later.

1. What advice would you give to Maurice and William?_____

_____

_____

_____

_____

_____

What Do You Do If You Are in an Accident?

Activity B   Name_____

Chapter 27   Date_____Period_____

If you are involved in an automobile accident, certain procedures need to be followed. Explain them below.

1. When involved in a car accident, you should: _____

_____

_____

_____

_____

_____

_____

_____

_____

_____

_____

_____

_____

_____

_____

_____

_____

_____

_____

_____

_____

_____

2. In some states, drivers are required by law to show proof of liability insurance if they are involved in an accident. Does your state require the proof of liability insurance coverage to be in the vehicle at all times?_____

_____

3. What type of auto liability insurance coverage is required in your state? _____

_____

4. If your state law requires proof of liability insurance coverage, what may happen to you if you do not have this proof of coverage? _____

_____

_____

Health Insurance

Activity C   Name_____

Chapter 27   Date_____ Period_____

Review the statements below and answer the questions that follow.

1. Spencer's arm was broken during a soccer game. He was taken to the hospital emergency room where his arm was X-rayed and set. The expenses were covered by his basic medical insurance. What other expenses does this type of insurance cover? _____

_____

_____

2. Mr. Conway had heart surgery, which involved very costly medical bills. Fortunately, the Conway family had major medical insurance coverage in addition to basic medical coverage. What are the advantages to this additional medical insurance? _____

_____

_____

3. Mrs. Ramos wants to be able to use any doctor or hospital she wants. What type of health care policy should she purchase? _____

_____

4. Marty had a sore throat and fever for two days. His parents are enrolled in an HMO through their company insurance. Where should Marty go for medical treatment?_____

   How much can Marty expect to pay at the HMO facility? _____

_____

5. Tawanda has joined a PPO through her employer. What should she consider when choosing a doctor? _

_____

_____

   How are the fees for medical service determined?_____

_____

_____

6. Nathaniel has a POS plan through his employer. How does a POS plan differ from an HMO plan? ____

_____

_____

   How will this affect Nathaniel's benefits? _____

7. What types of health insurance do you feel you should have? Explain._____

_____

_____

_____

_____

Home Insurance Possessions Inventory

Activity D

Chapter 27

Name_____

Date_____Period_____

For home insurance purposes, prepare an inventory of your household possessions and estimate their values. Include the model or serial number and brand name whenever possible. Then answer the questions that follow.

Inventory	
Item	**Estimated Value**

1. What is the difference between homeowner's insurance and renter's insurance? _____

_____

_____

2. Approximately how much home insurance coverage would you need to insure your possessions? _____

_____

3. What would be the advantage of having a large deductible? _____

_____

Insurance Terms to Know

Activity E

Chapter 27

Name_____

Date_____Period_____

Read the statements on the next page and write the missing terms in the crossword puzzle.

(Continued)

Name_____

Across

3. Health insurance that pays the largest share of expenses resulting from a major illness or serious injury. (two words)

6. This type of home insurance coverage insures you against such damages as fire and lightning, burglary and theft, vandalism, and explosions. (two words)

7. This life insurance covers the policyholder for a set period of time specified in the policy.

8. Auto insurance coverage that protects you if you are legally liable for an accident in which others are injured or killed. (three words)

11. A form of whole life insurance in which payments are limited to a set period of time.

12. A set amount of money paid to an insurance company on a regular basis in return for financial protection in the event a misfortune occurs that is covered by the policy.

15. Auto insurance coverage that pays for damages your car causes to the property of others if you are responsible for an accident. (three words)

16. This type of home insurance coverage protects you against financial loss if others are injured on or by your property, or if you or your property accidentally damages the property of others. (two words)

17. This life insurance covers the policyholder for a lifetime. (two words)

18. A type of health insurance that provides regular income payments when a person is unable to work for an extended period of time because of injury or illness.

19. Auto insurance coverage that pays for bodily injuries for which a hit-and-run driver is responsible. (two words)

20. Health insurance that covers the costs of hospitalization. (two words)

Down

1. Auto insurance coverage that pays for damage to your car caused by something other than another vehicle.

2. The amount you must pay before the insurance company will pay a claim.

4. A policyholder pays premiums throughout his or her life with this type of whole life policy. (two words)

5. Auto insurance coverage that pays for the damage to your car caused by a collision with another vehicle or object.

9. A plan to help people protect themselves from unexpected financial losses.

10. This property protection only covers damage or loss of personal property and possessions, not the dwelling itself. (two words)

13. Auto insurance coverage that pays for the medical expenses resulting from an accident regardless of who was at fault. (two words)

14. Auto insurance protection designed to eliminate the legal process of proving who is at fault in an accident. (two words)

Life Insurance

Activity F

Chapter 27

Name_____

Date_____Period_____

Indicate whether the statements are true or false by writing either *true* or *false* in the blanks. Then answer the following questions.

_____ 1. If you have no dependents, you really need life insurance.

_____ 2. When a life insurance policyholder dies, the insurance company pays the face value of the policy to the beneficiary.

_____ 3. Term insurance is a form of savings.

_____ 4. Whole life insurance covers the policyholder for a lifetime.

_____ 5. Premiums are higher on endowment policies because the cash value builds up faster.

_____ 6. Term insurance pays benefits only if the policyholder dies during the term of the policy.

_____ 7. Premiums for term insurance are higher than those for whole life insurance.

_____ 8. A renewable privilege allows the policyholder to review the policy at standard rates regardless of any changes in health.

_____ 9. Whole life insurance is simply for protection; it builds no cash value.

_____ 10. The beneficiary is the person named by the policyholder to receive the death benefit.

_____ 11. Universal life insurance does not allow flexibility in the premium payments.

_____ 12. When evaluating job offers, you need to consider the insurance programs the company offers.

_____ 13. The insurance company, agent, or policy you choose makes no difference in the coverage you receive or the premiums you pay.

14. What form of life insurance would you purchase if you supported a spouse? Explain. _____

_____

_____

15. What form of life insurance would you purchase if you had children? Explain. _____

_____

_____

16. What form of life insurance would you purchase if you had no dependents? Explain._____

_____

_____

17. What form of life insurance would you purchase if you supported elderly parents? Explain. _____

_____

_____

28 Managing Family, Work, and Citizenship Roles

Your Family Role

Activity A

Chapter 28

Name _____

Date _____ Period _____

Select someone in your class to interview. Ask the questions below about their family roles.

Name of Interviewee: _____

1. What is your current role in your family? _____

2. Have you had any other roles in the past? _____

3. What are your commitments to your family? _____

_____

_____

4. What household responsibilities do you handle as a family member? _____

_____

_____

5. How are the household chores assigned in your family? _____

_____

6. Do you consider your household assignments fair? Explain. _____

_____

_____

7. How would you assign household chores fairly? _____

_____

_____

8. What leisure activities do you share with family members? _____

_____

9. How do you balance the demands of family, school, and work? _____

_____

_____

10. How could you be more successful in handling your family roles? _____

_____

Managing Your Time

Activity B

Chapter 28

Name_____

Date_____Period_____

In order to balance your family and work roles, you need to plan and use your time wisely. List below the tasks you need to complete today. Then rank the top 10 tasks in order of priority. As you complete each task on the list, place a check in the space provided. At the end of the day, evaluate your plan by answering the questions at the bottom of the page.

Tasks for the day: _____

_____

_____

To-Do List

Done

_____   1. _____

_____   2. _____

_____   3. _____

_____   4. _____

_____   5. _____

_____   6. _____

_____   7. _____

_____   8. _____

_____   9. _____

_____ 10. _____

Did you waste any time? If so, how?_____

_____

How will you avoid time-wasters in the future?_____

_____

_____

During which tasks did you procrastinate?_____

_____

Were your deadlines realistic? Explain. _____

_____

_____

How did you stay motivated to complete the tasks? _____

_____

_____

Support Systems

Activity C

Chapter 28

Name_____

Date_____Period_____

Working with a partner, identify four support programs available in your community and describe them. Search the Internet, talk to friends and neighbors, read local newspapers, or contact local government offices to locate the groups that provide the programs. Report the results of your fact-finding below and be prepared to share your findings with the class.

Organization 1: _____

    Name of program: _____

    Target audience: _____

    Program description:_____

    _____

    _____

    _____

Organization 2: _____

    Name of program: _____

    Target audience: _____

    Program description:_____

    _____

    _____

    _____

Organization 3: _____

    Name of program: _____

    Target audience: _____

    Program description:_____

    _____

    _____

    _____

Organization 4: _____

    Name of program: _____

    Target audience: _____

    Program description:_____

    _____

    _____

    _____

Legal Terms

Activity D   Name_____

Chapter 28   Date_____Period_____

Complete the following sentences by filling in the blank.

_____ 1. When you _____ to vote, you add your name to a list of people who are allowed to vote.

_____ 2. _____ _____ govern the association between citizens and the government.

_____ 3. _____ _____ outline citizens' rights in relation to one another.

_____ 4. _____ _____ outline policies for dealing with foreign governments.

_____ 5. _____ _____ relate to the duties and powers of presidents and governors.

_____ 6. The purpose of _____ _____ is to protect society from offenses considered wrong and unjust.

_____ 7. _____ _____ establish the basic rights and freedoms of all citizens.

_____ 8. Murder, rape, or kidnapping would be considered a(n) _____.

_____ 9. Speeding or disorderly conduct would be considered a(n) _____.

_____ 10. A legally binding agreement between two or more people is a(n) _____.

_____ 11. In order for a contract to be _____, both parties must agree on the terms, be competent, be 18 years or older, and give consideration.

_____ 12. Persons entering into a contract are called _____.

_____ 13. A person who is able to understand the terms of a contract is considered _____.

_____ 14. _____ means each party must give up something in order to receive what the other party is offering.

_____ 15. A wrongful act committed against another person, independent of a contract, is a(n) _____.

Consulting a Lawyer

Activity E

Chapter 28

Name_____

Date_____Period_____

Answer the following questions about consulting a lawyer.

1. When you have an important financial or legal decision to make, when is the best time to consult a lawyer?

   _____

   _____

2. What are six examples of cases when a lawyer should be contacted? _____

   A. _____

   B. _____

   C. _____

   D. _____

   E. _____

   F. _____

3. How can you find a good lawyer?_____

   _____

   _____

4. What is the Lawyer Referral and Information Service (LRIS) and how can you locate it?_____

   _____

   _____

   _____

   _____

   _____

   _____

5. If you cannot afford to hire a lawyer, where might you find legal assistance for no or low cost?_____

   _____

   _____

6. Legal aid offices and clinics give advice in three main areas. What are they?_____

   _____

   _____

   _____

Examining the Court System

Activity F

Chapter 28

Name_____

Date_____Period_____

Answer the following questions about our court system.

1. What is the purpose of the court system? _____

_____

_____

_____

_____

2. What types of cases are tried by state courts?_____

_____

_____

3. What types of cases are tried by federal courts?_____

_____

_____

4. What factors determine the type of court in which a case will be tried? _____

_____

_____

_____

_____

5. Where is a court case first heard? _____

_____

_____

_____

6. What is a jury? _____

_____

7. What happens when a case is appealed? _____

_____

_____

8. What is the purpose of small claims court?_____

_____

9. Tyrone filed a lawsuit against Kate for breach of contract. Who is the plaintiff?_____

Who is the defendant?_____